Political Terrorism

PAUL WILKINSON

Lecturer in Politics, University College, Cardiff

D0369530

Macmillan

772303

© Government and Opposition 1974

All rights reserved. No part of this publication may
be reproduced or transmitted, in any form or by any
means, without permission.

First published 1974 by
THE MACMILLAN PRESS LTD
London and Basingstoke
Associated companies in New York Dublin
Melbourne Johannesburg and Madras

SBN 333 16812 7 (hard cover)
333 17469 0 (paper cover)

Printed in Great Britain by
THE ANCHOR PRESS LTD
Tiptree, Essex

For Rachel, John, and Charles

The paperback edition of this book is sold subject to the condition
that it shall not, by way of trade or otherwise, be lent, resold,
hired out, or otherwise circulated without the publisher's prior
consent in any form of binding or cover other than that in which
it is published and without a similar condition including this
condition being imposed on the subsequent purchaser.

STUDIES IN COMPARATIVE POLITICS

The purpose of the collection 'Studies in Comparative Politics' is to provide the students of politics with a series of up-to-date, short and accessible surveys of the progress of the discipline, its changing theoretical approaches and its methodological reappraisals.

The format of the individual volumes is understandably similar. All authors examine the subject by way of a critical survey of the literature on the respective subject, thus providing the reader with an up-to-date *bibliographie raisonnée* (either separate or contained in the text). Each author then proposes his own views on the future orientation. The style tries to bridge the often lamented gap between the highly specialised language of modern political science and the general reader. It is hoped that the entire collection will be of help to the students who try to acquaint themselves with the scholarly perspectives of contemporary politics.

S. E. Finer
Ghiţa Ionescu

Already published

A. H. BROWN: Soviet Politics and Political Science
BERNARD CRICK: Basic Forms of Government
C. H. DODD: Political Development
GHIŢA IONESCU: Comparative Communist Politics
DENNIS KAVANAGH: Political Culture
LESLIE J. MACFARLANE: Political Disobedience
W. J. M. MACKENZIE: The Study of Political Science Today
GEOFFREY K. ROBERTS: What is Comparative Politics?
WILLIAM WALLACE: Foreign Policy and the Political Process
PAUL WILKINSON: Political Terrorism
ROGER WILLIAMS: Politics and Technology
LESLIE WOLF-PHILLIPS: Comparative Constitutions

Forthcoming titles

S. E. FINER: The Study of Interest Groups

STUDIES IN COMPARATIVE POLITICS
published in association with
GOVERNMENT AND OPPOSITION

a quarterly journal of comparative politics, published by Government and Opposition Ltd, London School of Economics and Political Science, Houghton Street, London, WC2 2AE

EDITORIAL BOARD
Professor Leonard Schapiro, *University of London (Chairman)*
Professor David Apter, *Yale University, New Haven, Conn.*
Professor Bernard Crick, *University of London*
Professor Julius Gould, *University of Nottingham*
Professor James Joll, *University of London*
Dr Isabel de Madariaga, *University of London*

EDITOR
Professor Ghiţa Ionescu, *University of Manchester*

ADVISORY BOARD
Professor S. E. Finer, *University of Oxford (Chairman)*
Professor Daniel Bell, *Harvard University, Cambridge, Mass.*
Professor K. D. Bracher, *Bonn University*
Professor Robert A. Dahl, *Yale University, New Haven, Conn.*
F. W. Deakin, *St Antony's College, Oxford*
Professor Jacques Freymond, *Director of the Institut des Études Internationales, Geneva*
Professor Bertrand de Jouvenel, *Paris*
Professor Masao Maruyama, *University of Tokyo*
Asoka Mehta, *former Minister of Planning, New Delhi*
Professor John Meisel, *Queen's University, Kingston, Ontario*
Professor Ayo Ogunsheye, *University of Ibadan*
Professor Giovanni Sartori, *University of Florence*
Professor G. H. N. Seton-Watson, *University of London*
Professor Edward Shils, *University of Chicago and King's College, Cambridge*
Professor E. Tierno Galván, *late of the University of Salamanca*

Contents

Preface

The extended essay which follows is primarily concerned with the theoretical and comparative analysis of revolutionary terrorism, that is to say, with the use of terrorist tactics by revolutionary movements. It does not, however, exclude consideration of terroristic usages of war and the repressive terrorism of the state. Indeed it is argued here that each of these major sources of terror is intimately related both to the emergence of revolutionary terrorism and the conditions for its success or failure. Rather less space is given to the discussion of what we have termed 'sub-revolutionary' terrorism, that is to say, individual or isolated acts of terror which do not appear to be undertaken for revolutionary motives. In some, though by no means all, cases sub-revolutionary terrorism belongs to the realms of psychosis and crime rather than to political activism. This is not to deny that such acts may have unforeseen political consequences.

I should like to thank my College and my colleagues in the Department of Politics, Dr J. A. Cross, Mr R. E. Jones and Mrs G. Jones, for enabling me to spend the summer in British Columbia, where most of the book was planned and prepared. I owe a special debt to Professor Ghita Ionescu for encouraging me to write this book, and for his invaluable Editorial criticisms. My thanks also to the staffs of Simon Fraser University Department of History and the libraries at Simon Fraser, University of British Columbia, and University College, Cardiff, for their patience and assistance. The following are among those who have given generous encouragement and advice: Dr E. McWhinney, Simon Fraser University, Dr Leslie Paul, and Mr Richard Emery. My warmest thanks also to Mrs Sheila Spencer of University College, Cardiff, for typing the manuscript so meticulously, and to Mrs Elizabeth Bottomley of Macmillan. The faults and shortcomings of the book are, of course, the sole responsibility of the author. Last but not least, I thank my wife Susan for her invaluable help and for skilfully diverting three boisterous children.

December, 1973   P. W.

1 . Concepts of Terror and Terrorism

What do we mean when we speak of terror? In its most important and general sense the term signifies a psychic state of great fear or dread. Our modern words *terror*, *terrorise*, *terrible*, *terrorism*, and *deterrent*, are derived from the Latin verbs *terrere*, to tremble or to cause to tremble, and *deterrere*, to frighten from. The word *terror* also came to mean the action or quality of causing dread and, alternatively, a person, object or force, inspiring dread. Etymologists claim that the English terms *terrorism*, *terrorist*, and *terrorise* did not come into use until the equivalent French words *terrorisme*, *terroriste*, *terroriser* had developed in the revolutionary period between 1793 and 1798. Edmund Burke declaimed, 'Thousands of Hellhounds called Terrorists are let loose on the people.' The term *terrorist* came into general use to denote those revolutionaries who sought to use terror systematically either to further their views or to govern whether in France or elsewhere.

There is an almost infinite variety of events, phenomena, persons and objects that may, under certain conditions, strike terror into the hearts of human beings. Death and natural catastrophe have provided the common dreads of men and women throughout their history. Mankind's only final defence against the King of Terrors has been his beliefs in a form of life after death, his small cries of faith in the face of disaster. And, as if such fundamental terrors as volcanic eruption, flood, disease, starvation or attack by wild beasts were not enough, man invented his own systems of psychic terror, generally embodied in an awesome magical belief, myth and superstition, characteristically sustained by the secret societies, medicine men and shamans of many primitive peoples. In such systems the irrational basis of such nightmare terrors found its physical expression in, for example, human sacrifice for the propitiation of gods

9

and barbarous punishments for offences against the priestly codes. Typical of the devices used in such primitive systems of psychic terror were the masks of the American north-west Pacific Indian peoples who are the subject of a classic study by F. Boas.[1] In their strange ceremonies and festivals, dancers donned masks representing spirits, usually of wild animals. These would perform at night in the enclosed surroundings, illuminated solely by the light of fires, which appeared to bring the terrifying mask-creatures alive. By such means the Indians could be induced to believe in such spirits as the evil giant-woman goddess Tsonoqua of the Kwakiutl people, who was represented by a hideous black and white face with a twisted mouth. She was supposed to walk the forests carrying a large basket on her back to contain the bodies of the children she would eat. There is abundant historical and anthropological evidence[2] that such magico-religious beliefs and practices were capable of inducing states of psychic terror. Nor should we underestimate the extent of the human slaughter committed in the name of propitiating primitive gods. To cite only one example, even the worldly and warlike Bernal Díaz in his account of the conquest of New Spain ([31] pp. 132, 182)[3] expressed his horror at the piles of human skulls and bones of victims of cannibalistic sacrifice encountered at Xocotlan, Tlascala and elsewhere during the campaign of Cortés.

It does seem to be clear that magico-religious systems of psychic terror frequently do initiate and sustain practices of physical terrorisation which in effect tend to both reinforce the institutionalisation and ideological legitimation of terroristic violence. Yet it is important to observe that states of psychic terror among individuals and groups may be induced by an entirely irrational fear or dread or wild rumour. In cases of a purely subjective psychosis of this nature it may be an extremely

[1] F. Boas, 'The Social Organization and the Secret Societies of the Kwakiutl Indians', *Annual Report of the Smithsonian Institution* (Washington, D.C., 1895).

[2] For a discussion of this evidence see Paul Radin's useful book, *The World of Primitive Man* (New York: Grove Press, 1960) ch. 6 ff.

[3] Numbers in square brackets refer to the Bibliography, pp. 152–60.

difficult task, even for psychiatric and psychological experts, to discover, and to dispose of, individual burdens of Fear. In order to set about this they must identify the psychological origins of the fear itself.[4] One of the most difficult tasks of all may be to eliminate both subjective and collective psychoses which have been inaugurated and socialised by intensive indoctrination of a religious or ideological nature. It is true that evidence concerning adults subjected to short-term campaigns of indoctrination shows that they are only superficially and briefly influential on the personality. On the other hand, it would be absurd to discount the importance of long-term effects of intensive and continuous indoctrination of individuals, throughout childhood and adolescence, on personality development. For example, can it be seriously doubted that most individuals schooled entirely under the crushing force of Jesuit propaganda described so vividly by James Joyce in *A Portrait of the Artist as a Young Man* would continue to believe in the terrors of hell-fire? Terror, whether it be terror of Divine punishment or retribution or terror of the decrees of the Party or of the Law, has been seen as functionally desirable if not essential by many leaders and rulers throughout history.

Nor is it the case that scientific positivism, rationalism and mass education have eliminated at a stroke irrational and bizarre fears. In all communities there are some individuals with Thurberish fears of electricity 'leaking' or of being invaded by armies of intruding burglars. And there are always others who seem positively to enjoy terrorising themselves in an orgy of vicarious horror through films or books. The point to be made here is that these various forms of psychic terror, whether self-induced or stimulated by art, religion, or indoctrination, are not the main concern of the present study. Our main concern is with political terror: that is to say with the use of coercive intimidation by revolutionary movements, regimes or individuals for political motives.

It is, however, important to bear in mind that terror is in the heart and mind of the victim, it is a *subjective* experience. Individual reactions to terroristic experiences will vary according to

[4] See Freud [44 45] for an early discussion of the social effects of psychosis.

11

their individual psychology and situation. This basic fact of the wide variation in individuals' tolerance or susceptibility for terror makes nonsense of the claims of some terrorists that terror can be a rational, selective, discriminate political weapon of real precision. Quite apart from the fact that terrorists frequently hit the innocent by mistake, and by design, it is extraordinarily difficult for terrorists to predict the psychological reactions of that sector of the population which they regard as their 'audience'. Nor are we entitled to accept at face value the claims made by all perpetrators of political terror that they are using extreme violence in a rationally calculated and systematic manner. Some individuals, leaders and groups become so possessed by fanatical hatred or consumed by desire for vengeance that they create mass terror by acts of genocide and massacre. Their victims are no less terrorised by this mass terror than those who live out their lives terrorised under a system of oppression and slavery: the difference between them is one of time-scale. There is, however, one important difference between political terror and the other forms of terror we have mentioned: outside the pages of science fiction it is impossible to conceive of an actual political terror which does not resort to extreme violence against the person (in the sense of destructive harm). The political terrorists always resort to political murder in order to induce the psychic state of terror. In other words for political terror to be effective a purely psychic threat is not sufficient. To the extent that its victims can recognise that they are physically threatened by a political faction, movement or regime, individuals' states of terror may be seen to have a perfectly rational basis.

Just as it is important to distinguish between political terror and other sources of purely psychic terror, we must also differentiate it from the purely criminal variety. Criminal terrorists may employ blackmail and intimidation alone in order to enrich themselves: for instance the professional blackmailer may be able to induce a state of psychic terror by words alone. Political terrorists almost invariably combine psychic terror, for example blackmail and defamation, with physical violence and threats of violence. More fundamental is the difference in their objectives. Criminal individuals or groups resort to terrorising their victims with the sole object of selfish material gain or of eliminating a possible rival or informer. The vast majority of crimes are certainly not motivated by any social or political purpose. For the political terrorist proper, however, it is a *sine qua non* that the overriding objective and ultimate justification for terror is the furtherance of his political cause. We shall, however, have cause to analyse in more detail later the reasons for the often close affinity and linkage between types of terrorism under certain conditions. Though the socio-economic and political aspects of banditry have been closely considered in a recent study,[5] the exploitation of professional criminal groups and methods by political organisations has been little discussed. Apart from the well-known individual cases of corruption among elected office holders in both democratic and autocratic regimes, there is the phenomenon of the exploitation of criminal methods by political movements seeking either to supplement their funds by means of expropriation or by protection rackets, in order to obtain weapons or simply to augment their armed strength in a period of internal war.[6]

It would be useful to attempt a clearer definition of the general characteristics of political terror and terrorism by means of conceptual clarification, and by drawing upon the very few recent scholarly discussions of the conceptual problems. A major characteristic of political terror is its indiscriminate nature. This is not to deny that terrorists generally have a specific human 'target', whether individual or collective, which they intend shall be the victim of the most direct physical harm. Quite apart from the physical danger of persons who are not pre-selected targets being hurt there is the unavoidable side effect of widespread fear that others might be harmed. As Raymond Aron remarks in one of his most percipient observations on terror: 'An action of violence is labelled "terrorist" when its psychological effects are out of proportion to its purely physical result. In this sense, the so-called indiscriminate acts of revolutionaries are terrorist, as were the Anglo-American zone bomb-

[5] On the history of phenomena of banditry, see Eric Hobsbawm [59].

[6] For a collection of useful approaches to the study of internal war, see Harry Eckstein [34].

ings. The lack of discrimination helps to spread fear, for if no one in particular is a target, no one can be safe' ([6] p. 170). Terrorists are frequently prepared to engage in the indiscriminate murder of civilians. All men, women, and children, regardless of their role or position in society, may be regarded as potential victims for the sake of the 'cause'. As a policy the waging of terror necessarily involves disregarding the rules and conventions of war: non-combatants, hostages, prisoners-of-war, and neutrals have no inviolable rights in their eyes.

It is also characteristic of acts of terror that they appear entirely unpredictable and arbitrary to the society which suffers them. One writer has expressed this point very clearly: '. . . no observance of commands – no matter how punctilious – on the part of the prospective victims can ensure their safety' (S. Andreski, 'Terror', in [48]). There are of course many instances of the individual victims of terroristic assassination or mass murder being given preliminary warning that they are to die. The point is that such acts are only 'selective' and 'predictable' according to the rationalisations of the terrorists. As Malraux writes 'le terroriste décidât seul exécutât seul' ([94] p. 189), and it is in this sense true to describe terrorism as a peculiar kind of tyranny in which the potential victim is unable to do anything to avoid his destruction because the terrorist is operating and judging on the basis of his own idiosyncratic code of norms and values. Do these characteristics of unpredictability and arbitrariness also apply in the case of the repressive terror of the state? There are two major reasons why they are common also to state terror. First, leaders and agencies of force in the state, who have acquired the preponderance of coercive power, may disregard the underlying values and norms of the existing law with impunity within their domain. Secondly, tyrannical dictators or totalitarian governments tend in the process of consolidating their power to subvert and manipulate the legal structure in order to forge it into a weapon of oppression of their internal opponents. Under such conditions, instead of the sovereignty of the state and the rule of law being used solely to apply punishment for clearly defined crimes or offences, judicial acts may become what Hobbes termed acts of hostility. For Hobbes a hostile act 'falls not under the name of Punishment' ([57] p. 241) because it is an act against one who is not politically obedient to the legal authority (i.e. the state). Punishment, argues Hobbes, is reserved for those citizens of a state who have broken the law. It is 'an Evill inflicted by publique authority . . . to the end that the will of men may thereby better be disposed to obedience' ([57] p. 238). But in response to an act of hostility, he claimed, 'all infliction of evil is lawfull' ([57] p. 241), that is there are no limits to the violence that can be committed. It is clear that many tyrannies and terrorisms have sought to confuse this important distinction by lending their actions a quasi-legal rationale. They resort to defining any action they choose as an act of political disobedience, thus claiming that by their hostile acts they are in reality punishing political crimes. We shall have cause later to note the institutionalisation and ideological rationalisation of the relationship between the practice of terror and the legal systems of many repressive regimes.

Political terror can also be differentiated from other forms of violence, agitation, intimidation and coercion by virtue of its extreme and ruthlessly destructive methods. These may range from genocide, massacre and political murder and torture at one end of the scale of violence, to physical beatings, harassment and defamation campaigns at the other. For any large-scale campaign of repressive or of revolutionary terror, the terrorists find it necessary to arm themselves adequately to check any possible resistance. Whereas spears and machetes were once adequate weapons in African tribal regimes of terror, and the famous sect of the Assassins in the eleventh and twelfth centuries used the dagger, modern terrorists must depend upon a minimal supply of guns and explosives. The factor of dependence upon weaponry, combined with the reliance of many terrorist movements and agencies upon a military organisational structure and style, underlines the close relationship between terrorism and war. Indeed, many American and French scholars have been so impressed by this affinity that they have tended to study terror exclusively in the context of 'internal war' and problems of 'counter-insurgency' [63, 92, 93, 112, 134, 136].

It is in practice extremely difficult to draw clear boundaries between war and terror. E. V. Walter, in his pioneering socio-

15

logical analysis of the regime of terror, argues that, unlike civil terror, military terror aims ultimately at exterminating the enemy. Civil terror, he asserts, is always an instrument of power aimed at the control and not destruction of the population: 'When violence is employed in the service of power, the limit of force is the destruction of the thing that is forced' ([145] p. 14). But there are two serious confusions in Walter's argument. Firstly, we cannot assume that all wars are wars of extermination: even in modern wars distinctions are sometimes made between the civilian population and the armed forces of protagonists, and one of the normal strategic objectives is still the acquisition and control of enemy territories and their inhabitants. Secondly, and more important, internal revolutionary and state terror can both be directed at the deliberate destruction of whole social groups who have been designated as enemies. Terrorists may believe such a policy of liquidation to be necessary in order to capture or sustain their political control, or it may be dictated by ideological reasons, or it may derive from motives of hatred, vengeance or even sadism or mass hysteria, or a combination of these factors. The point to be made is that, historically, acts of civil terror have not, unfortunately, always stopped short at the subjugation of certain real or imagined opponents. Totalitarian regimes of terror have committed crimes against humanity on a vast scale. We have no right to assume that the perpetrators of civil terror will arrive by some rational calculation at a notional limit to violence, and that they will always rule out extermination. As for the implications for political control, mass murders will intensify rather than extinguish the general terror: everyone in the population will be terrified lest they be caught in the next wave of terror. Thus, although this book does not attempt a detailed analysis of war terror (i.e. terroristic usages in military conflict), our discussion must necessarily include consideration of the many kinds of destruction against the civil population which can be understood as what Hobbes called 'hostile acts', or acts of war against the population.

What fundamentally distinguishes terrorism from other forms of organised violence is not simply its severity but its features of amorality and antinomianism. Terrorists either profess indifference to existing moral codes or else claim exemption from all such obligations. Political terror, if it is waged consciously and deliberately, is implicitly prepared to sacrifice all moral and humanitarian considerations for the sake of some political end. Ideologies of terrorism assume that the death and suffering of those who are innocent of any crime are means entirely justified by their political ends. In their most explicit and candidly amoral form such terrorist rationalisations amount to a Nietzschean doctrine of the Will to Power. Might is right; terror can always be justified as the expediency of the strong; and such Judaeo-Christian notions as mercy, compassion and conscience must go with the weak to the wall of history. Political terror is not always justified in such explicit terms. Some utopian or messianic sects and movements that have resorted to terror have attempted a teleological justification, generally involving the rejection of all existing ethical principles and codes on the grounds that morality is manipulated in the interests of the rulers. In some cases it is argued that the acts of terror are necessary sacrifices to be made on the journey towards introducing a new revolutionary order which will introduce a New Man and a New Order and, of course, a Revolutionary Morality. But, of course, the first task is that the existing order and morality are destroyed.

We have thus identified some of the key characteristics common to all forms of political terror: indiscriminateness, unpredictability, arbitrariness, ruthless destructiveness and the implicitly amoral and antinomian nature of a terrorist's challenge. There remains the important distinction between political terror and political terrorism. Clearly political terror may occur in isolated acts and also in the form of extreme, indiscriminate and arbitrary mass violence, the kind of insurrectionary outburst that characterised the lynchings and sackings at the height of the popular terror in parts of revolutionary France. Such terror is not systematic, it is unorganised and is often impossible to control. 'Therefore neither one isolated act, nor a series of random acts is terrorism' ([63] p. 384). Political terrorism, properly speaking, is a sustained policy involving the waging of organised terror either on the part of the state, a movement or faction, or by a small group of individuals. Systematic terrorism invariably entails some organisational

17

structure, however rudimentary, and some kind of theory or ideology of terror. One of the earliest attempts to clarify the concept of terrorism in modern social science defined it as 'the method or the theory behind the method whereby an organised group or party seeks to achieve its avowed aims chiefly through the systematic use of violence' [55]. Perhaps the fact that the 1968 edition of the *International Encyclopaedia of the Social Sciences*[7] does not even include an entry on terrorism indicates that its editors were satisfied with Hardman's definition. In any case we shall argue that it is a very valuable operational definition. It will be helpful to refer later to some of the useful insights contained in Hardman's early analysis.

A more recent attempt at definition of terrorism, still quite influential in the American literature, is that of Thornton [136]. His working definition stresses what he terms the 'symbolic' character of terrorist acts: 'Thus, in an internal war situation, terror is a symbolic act designed to influence political behaviour by extra-normal means, entailing the use or threat of violence' ([136] p. 73). We have already agreed upon the importance of extra-normal means and the use of violence in defining the characteristics of terror. The most questionable element in Thornton's statement is the claim that all acts of terror in an internal war are deliberately propagandist acts, by which he means that they are always designed to convey a message, sign or warning to either their opponents, the 'neutral' population or to those who belong to or sympathise with the terrorist movement. Now this patently is not the case with all terrorist acts: it is true that many terrorist assassinations of major public figures or representatives of law and order have a propagandist and an intimidatory aim. Terrorists may aim, through such actions, to advertise the existence of their cause and to signify their willingness to fight for it, and inspire popular support. Or they may be employed to intimidate a particular sector of the population, to 'warn' against collaboration with the government or with the terrorists' opponents, or to implant a sense of insecurity and fear in a specific group such as the police. These symbolic and propagandist functions of terror acts may be rather more important in the early stages of insurgency. But, as

[7] (New York: Collier-Macmillan, 1968).

Thornton goes on to point out in his useful analysis of terrorist tactics, terrorism is by no means confined to the preliminary stages of insurgency. Moreover, both in the preliminary and later stages of an insurgents' campaign, terrorist acts are very often deployed for political purposes other than conveying 'messages' or 'warnings'. Terrorists engaged in a struggle for power often turn their terror against rivals, both within and outside their movements, and many of their acts of assassination, murder, 'execution', 'punishment', 'expropriation' of cash or arms, kidnappings, etc., are undertaken for reasons of expediency and are deliberately clandestine. Attempts are often made to remove even the suspicion of a movement's complicity in such acts by attempting to pin responsibility on a rival movement or on the authorities. It is therefore too constricting and misleading to count as terror only those acts whose objectives are symbolic. In the later stages of terrorist struggle, particularly, objectives are likely to be dictated more by the military necessities of weakening the security forces and lowering their efficiency, and by the need to protect both the terrorists and their bases and supply dumps from capture.

The difficulties encountered in Thornton's definition help to emphasise the very real problems of distinguishing clearly between political terrorism and the phenomena of intimidation, psychological warfare and defamation which very often, though not invariably, accompany it. A useful attempt has been made to distinguish political terrorism from intimidation:

Intimidation differs from terrorism in that the intimidator . . . merely threatens injury or material harm in order to arouse fear of severe punishment for non-compliance with his demands. . . . The attitude of the political terrorist is entirely different. He imposes the punishment meted out by his organization upon those who are considered guilty or who are held to interfere with the revolutionary programme; thus he serves notice that his organization will be satisfied with nothing short of the removal of the undesired social or governmental system and of the persons behind it. The terrorist does not threaten; death or destruction is part of his programme of action . . . ([55] p. 576).

19

Psychological warfare methods, as Roucek pointed out ([118] pp. 169–70), have been part of military knowledge since at least the fifth century B.C. when Sun Tzu's *The Book of War* described how the enemy could be thrown into confusion by the use of strange noises, numerous banners and surprise attacks. Napoleon was one of the many great military commanders who understood the importance of the psychological factor: he claimed, 'the moral is to the physical in war as three to one'. Roucek also draws attention to the heightened opportunities for psychological intimidation afforded by simultaneous acts of physical terror, for example, by means of the publication of lists of those sentenced to death and those already executed, and by organising public executions. Nevertheless, there is a real distinction, unfortunately not made clear in Roucek's article, between psychological warfare proper and acts of political terrorism.

It is also very important to be clear that all forms of civil violence do not necessarily involve political terrorism. The just war legitimated by the medieval Thomist philosophers was not envisaged as a warrant for indiscriminate destruction, the murder of non-combatants or of victory by any means. Nor does revolutionary insurrection or rebellion inevitably produce terrorism, and indeed the Thomists followed Marsilio of Padua in believing in the feasibility of a just rebellion. And from antiquity, of course, the act of tyrannicide was another form of civil violence considered entirely legitimate, even heroic and praiseworthy. For example, after the two Athenian friends, Aristogeiton and Harmodius, were executed following an unsuccessful attempt on the life of the tyrant Hippias, their descendants were given special privileges and the two friends became legendary heroes. Tyrannicide came to be seen in almost religious terms as an act of sacred duty aimed at removing the evil of the tyrannical ruler. Indiscriminate terror can never, in principle, be morally justified. But conversely many acts of rebellion, insurgency, and regular or irregular war which do not involve indiscriminate terrorisation of the population, and which may be shown to be morally justified, are often erroneously labelled as terrorist acts by opposing parties.

We have attempted the following conceptual clarifications:

(i) to distinguish political terror from terror in general, (ii) to define political terrorism, and (iii) to distinguish both political terror and terrorism from other forms of civil violence (some of which are closely akin to political terrorism and may sometimes accompany it). Now it has been a central theme of our conceptual discussion that moral and evaluative considerations are integrally involved. The student of terrorism, therefore, has constantly to be on his guard against polemical usages of the term. Thus, in attempting to determine whether a specific action (or series of actions) is terroristic or not, the scholar should be aware that he is making a value judgement about the perpetrators of the alleged act, and about the circumstances of their actions.

Historical judgements of this kind can only be made on the basis of carefully authenticated empirical evidence. It need hardly be added that such evidence is not always available. What is being admitted here is the evaluative nature of the concept of terrorism employed in the present discussion. The corollary is that the debate as to the ethical justification in a specific case both arises from, and runs parallel with, the continuing empirical inquiry. Naturally those who are prepared to condone the means of terrorism are generally ready to provide a rationale for such acts in other terms, for example, political expediency, ideological or historical necessity.

SOME ETHICAL CONSIDERATIONS

As we shall have cause to note frequently in our analysis there is a constant tension apparent in the literature on terrorism between judgement and prescription and the presumed demands of scientific impartiality or historical objectivity. Some writers point to the close affinities of terror with totalitarianism and tyranny. Some have pointed to the corrupting effects of terror upon its perpetrators as well as its costs for society as a whole and the sufferings of its victims. Modern social scientists writing on the subject appear extremely nervous of entering the ethical debate on terrorist practices and ideology. When they do so it is in an almost *sotto voce* parenthetical fashion to state their objections on social or political grounds, and very rarely to make any clear cut condemnation on moral grounds. For example,

21

In this writer's opinion, terrorism is socially as well as poli-
cally unacceptable, as the following ways in which acts of
terrorism may be extraordinary should demonstrate. Acts of
terrorism are often particularly atrocious and psychologically
shocking, such as throat-cutting or physical mutilation of
victims. . . . The act is not only unpredictable but often
anonymous. This arbitrariness of terrorist violence makes it
unacceptable and abnormal ([63] p. 385).

Dallin and Breslauer claim that 'our attempt here to deal with
terror as a phenomenon that can be rationally analyzed in no
way implies any moral indifference or callousness toward its
human impact or social costs' ([28] p. x). The present study is
at least partly concerned with the appalling human and social
costs of terrorism whoever its perpetrators and whatever its
ideological motivation. It is, firstly, concerned to attempt to
understand the motivations and objectives of terrorists and to
identify the kinds of political, socio-economic and cultural conditions that nurture and sustain terror. It is, secondly, concerned
to identify what possible prophylactic political, social or economic measures might be taken to prevent it. Thirdly, it considers
what effective anti-terrorist actions of a short-term nature
should be undertaken, particularly by constitutional democratic
governments which are already subject to terrorist attack.

We need make no apology for this prophylactic concern in our
study of terrorist theory, ideology, and practice. It is possible,
after all, to point to a long and distinguished tradition of
classical political theory concerning corruptions and mal-
formations in political life and organisation. The classical
Socratic teaching on tyranny, for example, dealt with both the
pathology of tyranny as a form of government and with the
therapeutics through which the evils of tyranny might be alle-
viated (cf. [131]). Apart from candidly admitting our moral
disapproval of terrorism, there are two general strategies we can
adopt in order to ensure that, as far as is possible, our comparative historical analysis is relatively balanced and sympathetic to
the dilemmas of individuals and groups involved.

First we must deal adequately with the elementary fact that
many states, as well as movements and factions, have employed

terror. They have used it for repression of their own citizens, political opponents, and minorities, as well as against conquered peoples and enemies in war. Roucek has noted how 'the most horrible forms of brutality have been sanctioned for the use of the legal authorities' ([118] p. 168). He quotes Charles Merriam's catalogue of a few of these devices used by the state: 'Restraint, the lash, torture in many forms, mutilation, humiliation, isolation, exile . . . death. . . . The rack, the boot, branding, the dungeon, the "hellhole", boiling water and molten metal, crucifixion, burnings, sawing and pulling asunder . . .' ([100] p. 135). Moreover, the terror of the state is very often historically antecedent to revolutionary terrorism. What makes Brian Crozier's use of the term 'counter-terror' to designate the terror used by the state against insurgents so misleading is precisely the implication that the state does not initiate the cycle of terror. What Crozier and others have rightly drawn attention to [27, 56, 136] are the phenomena of official state departments charged with mounting terrorist-style offensives against insurgent terrorist organisations. During the Second World War, for example, Nazi Germany organised 'gangs' to hunt out partisan units in areas such as Yugoslavia by emulating even their clothing and mode of life before finding and destroying them. More recently we have the example of Mivtah Elohim (meaning 'God's Wrath'), an Israeli-government specialist terror squad which raided Beirut in April 1973 and killed three Palestine guerrilla leaders and over a dozen other people.[8]

Now when a country such as Israel, which is a liberal democracy, practises a deliberate policy of counter-terror, important moral issues immediately arise. Many Israelis would feel completely justified in supporting the Israeli attack. They would do so on the grounds of one of the most frequently used justifications, that is, that it was a necessary act of self-defence. After all, they argue, the squad did succeed in killing three known Palestinian terrorist leaders. If certain innocent bystanders got in the way then this was just a pity. Here, it is important to realise, is a clear instance of one of the most popularly appealing and widespread arguments in justification for terror, *the morality*

[8] See the report on the Beirut raid in *The Times*, 12 April 1973.

of the just vengeance, or 'an eye for an eye and a tooth for a tooth'.

There is another line of argument used to justify limited or isolated acts of terror under extremely rare circumstances, a defence quite different from the argument of a *morality of just vengeance.* This is the *theory of the lesser evil.* Let us assume that a state or a community is confronted by an enemy state or force so corrupted by evil, so physically mighty and so ruthlessly terroristic in its methods of war that it cannot be destroyed by any conventional means. Under these conditions it is argued there may be an opportunity of ridding the world of this greater evil by the lesser evil of a crushing and terrible demonstration of force. This is the kind of argument often used to defend the decision to drop atomic bombs on Hiroshima and Nagasaki. A macabre debate about a kind of 'quantitative morality' tends to ensue. How far can one calculate whether the demonstration of terror will be final? What if the blow leads to a further retaliatory spiral? On what basis can one weigh the relative 'cost' in innocent victims of the final blow with the possible costs of continuing conflict by other means? It must be admitted that the very terms of this kind of debate are repugnant to the values of many people. Yet they are matters of serious practical consequence to specialists in nuclear strategy and theory of nuclear deterrence. The top half of Herman Kahn's well-known escalation ladder is after all a scenario of terror of unimaginable proportions [68]. It is worth bearing in mind that there are many strategic theorists and military men who are daily professionally involved in the rationalities of super-terror.

Two other general arguments are often used by terrorists to defend their actions. The first is that no other means were available to their movement or group; there were no representative institutions, free media or other means of making non-violent political progress for their cause, or else they were denied access to them, or if they gained access they were baulked by an intransigent executive or (in the case of a colonial people) by the metropolitan government of the controlling power. Now in some cases this kind of argument can be found to be based on overwhelming political evidence, and whether one disapproves of terrorism on moral grounds or not one must face up to the very compelling nature of the *ultima ratio* argument, the argument that terror is the only weapon left to the revolutionary *in extremis*. This kind of argument is very often combined with a second major justification claiming that terrorism has proved to be tactically 'successful' in similar conditions to one's own, and that therefore it can also bring one victory. Here the argument concerning moral justification is linked directly with problems of empirical evidence to which we will be devoting attention mainly in this study. What criteria can we adopt to test the 'success' or 'failure' of a political terrorist campaign? Under what conditions is it possible to predict the 'success' of terrorist tactics as either the primary method, or as a subsidiary weapon, in attaining political objectives? Is there any practicable means of assessing the costs and benefits that may be involved in attaining political victory by terrorism? In this kind of argument, which we shall be examining in detail later in relation to practices and ideologies of terror, we see the importance of emulation, of influential models or scenarios of revolution. There is abundant evidence to show that they can exert an appeal, a promise of victory, which can effectively override, for many movement participants, the restraints imposed by the moral and religious codes of their societies. It is useful to recognise the force of these appeals even though, in a specific case, we may find grounds to doubt the truth of terrorists' claims that *no other means* were available to them.

Another major set of issues to be confronted in considering the ethical aspects of terrorism is whether acts of political terrorism are to be equated with crimes. In what sense are they comparable with or analogous to crimes either morally or legally? Most acts of terrorist violence – such as assassination, wounding, arson, destruction of property, etc. – are of course defined as crimes under the legal codes of all states. Sometimes those who are brought to trial and charged with such offences freely admit responsibility for committing the acts, for which they face conviction and often a heavy penalty. In such cases the accused normally use the trial as an opportunity to publicise the political objectives which they claim to be the sole motive behind their actions. Generally, political terrorists will claim (i) that they do

25

not recognise the legality or legitimacy of the court which tries them and (ii) that their actions, if admitted to, are justified as being pure deeds of revolution designed to bring down an evil and corrupted political and social order. Their judges and not the accused are the real criminals in their eyes. This stance of the political terrorist may seem to be particularly unreasonable in the circumstances of trials in constitutional democracies where the rule of law, independence of judiciary, and safeguards of due process and legal rights of the accused are the norm. In a sense there can be no true dialogue, under these conditions, between the official representatives of the system and those who deny their legitimacy. It is clear, however, that in these circumstances, the truly impartial court could not condone or take a specially lenient view of the actions of terrorists simply on the grounds that their crimes were politically motivated. It is a matter of record that in some cases the government will bring discreet pressure on the judicial branch to pass severe or exemplary punishments where an alleged revolutionary conspiracy against the state is regarded by the government as a serious threat.

Far more complex moral issues arise where the terroristic acts of the state are involved. It has long been understood that even liberal constitutional governments may, either premeditatedly or by default, perform tyrannical or despotic acts. Burke drew attention to the danger: '. . . it is not perhaps so much by the assumption of unlawful powers, as by the unwise or unwarrantable use of those which are most legal, that governments oppose their true end and object, for there is such a thing as tyranny as well as usurpation.'[9] There are abundant historical examples of terroristic acts being performed by the civil, military, or security forces of liberal democratic states (for example, by certain French interrogators and policemen in Algeria, by certain U.S. soldiers and units in Vietnam and by certain individual members of British security forces operating in Africa and south-east Asia). It is true, of course, that such actions are never undertaken with the prior consent and explicit authority of democratic opinion and government as a

[9] Speech on a motion for leave to bring in a bill to repeal and alter certain Acts respecting religious opinions.

26

whole. Such acts of terror are not normally the subject of public boasts or cloaked in a spurious political legitimacy by parliamentary enactment. They normally take the form of abuse of delegated powers, and those involved often conspire together desperately lest details of their acts of terror should be the subject of inquiry at a higher level. They are obsessed with keeping their actions secret precisely because they know that under the constitutional codes of the liberal-democratic states they may be called to account for their crimes. Individuals guilty of such crimes under a democracy may not therefore deny that their terrorist acts of murder or brutality are contrary to the law, but they can and often do plead either ignorance of the law, or that in committing such acts they were merely carrying out 'superior orders'. It is surely possible to envisage individuals being bullied or coerced into committing acts of terror, but does this absolve the 'unwilling' perpetrators from all moral responsibility?

The dilemmas of individual moral responsibility become enormously intensified and indeed almost inescapable under totalitarian dictatorship such as the Third Reich. The theory of *raison d'état* has, of course, often been invoked by all kinds of states in order to justify acts of state which are generally regarded as crimes. Such acts are defended on the grounds that they are *imperative* measures in order to assure the survival of the state itself and its legal order. But supposing the sovereignty of the state is perverted for the purposes of crime and terror? Suppose it attempts to garb crimes against humanity in the cloak of legality? Hannah Arendt has made a profound and erudite contribution to the debate on this very problem ([3] pp. 253 ff.). She argues that in the case of Nazi war criminals, the legal defences of 'acts of state' and 'superior orders' must break down. Her argument implies that those ordered to participate in massacres under the decrees of such a state are criminals in the moral sense unless they refuse to obey. We are led back to a Thomist argument that when a tyrannical ruler orders the ruled to perform evil acts, disobedience is a moral duty. Presumably the ultimate basis for individual judgement in such extreme circumstances must be a more fundamental natural moral law which overrides the law of states. In such situations it is hard not to agree with Arendt's conclusion that all the individual citizen is left with as a rule of conduct is his individual 'instinctual' moral sense of right or wrong. Indeed, on what other basis could the judges at the Nuremberg tribunal or the judges of Eichmann at Jerusalem determine responsibility for 'crimes against humanity'? These dreadful crimes of genocide, persecution and what Arendt terms 'administrative massacre' were committed in accordance with decrees and regulations, as Eichmann never tired of pointing out, laid down by the Nazi state. They were, nevertheless, crimes in the fundamental moral sense of being evil acts aimed at the destruction of the spirit, status and dignity of the human person.

Terrorists have often found ideological or political rationalisations ready to hand to justify their acts whether in the name of the Revolution, the Revolutionary Party, Freedom, Equality and Solidarity, or for national liberation, defence or glory. Roads to Utopia are strewn with the bodies of their victims: 'O Liberté! O Liberté! que de crimes on commet en ton nom.'[10] There is even a special ideology of nihilistic terror, which we shall examine more closely, which deliberately promotes crimes of terror and destruction as a means of sowing social despair and collapse. Dostoyevsky's fictional character Verkhovensky (supposedly modelled on the terrorist Nechayev) puts the nihilist case for crime concisely in a conversation with Stavrogin: 'When I went abroad, Littre's theory that crime is insanity was the vogue; when I returned, crime was no longer insanity, but just commonsense, indeed, almost a duty, and, at any rate, a noble protest. "How can an educated man be expected to refrain from killing his victim if he must have money?" But this is only a beginning' ([33] p. 421).

We may conclude by summing up this brief discussion of some ethical considerations. Acts of terror are frequently committed by individuals or movements in defiance or disregard of prevailing legal code. In many other instances acts of terror, including some of the worst cases of mass terror, have been condoned, promoted and committed by agencies of the state. If all political terrorism can be said to entail moral crime we

[10] Words of Mme Roland (1754–93) on passing the statue of Liberty while *en route* for the scaffold.

must recognise the fact that this includes many crimes sanctioned by law.

THE STUDY OF POLITICAL TERRORISM

It is hardly necessary to draw attention to the contemporary relevance of the study of political terrorism. Some indication of the scale of current concern to increase our knowledge of terrorism and how it might be contained is demonstrated by the intensive activity of governments and national organisations in organising study groups, conventions, and inquiries into the subject. The United Nations, the Socialist International, the International Society of Jurists, the United States government and the British Association for the Advancement of Science have all recently sponsored contributions to the growing debate on the subject. However variable the quality of this discussion, its burgeoning is in itself of some interest and is surely partly a reflection on the dramatic increase in the incidence of terrorist acts (particularly international terrorism such as aircraft hijacking and the kidnapping of diplomats) in the late 1960s.[11] It is noteworthy that terrorist acts are by no means exclusively, or even predominantly, the phenomena of developing countries. There is considerable evidence of its increase in the so-called advanced and 'post-industrial' societies.

After an initial flourish of interest among historians and political scientists in the inter-war period it must be admitted that political terrorism has been a neglected subject of study among political scientists and social scientists generally. Following the pioneer works of Spiridovich [127] and Waciorski [143] there was a very long gap before any further comparative analyses or general histories were produced. Notable exceptions are Feliks Gross's study *The Seizure of Political Power* [51] and the earlier work by Arendt which dealt in part with the terror of totalitarian regimes [4]. One of the pioneering British contributions to the literature was by the freelance political analyst Brian Crozier, who published his well-known study of post-1945 insurrections, *The Rebels* [27], in 1960. It was not until 1969 that a full-length study of the sociology of terror, with special reference to native African regimes of terror, appeared, and

[11] For figures on the escalation of aircraft hijacking see p. 123.

most of the burgeoning American literature on counter-insurgency and revolutionary terrorism dates from the mid and late 1960s. There has been very little foundation-backed research into terrorism in the United States, and almost none in Britain or in Europe generally. E. V. Walter's claim that 'this form of power remains at the edges of rational enquiry, but the experience of recent times, punctuated by terroristic outbreaks and burdened by regimes of terror, makes the world tremble with an awareness that seeks general explanations' ([145] p. 3) remains a largely unheeded *cri de cœur*. It has been voiced again recently by Dallin and Breslauer who state, 'We soon discovered, to our surprise, that the theoretical literature on political terror was not nearly so well developed as we had expected and that, in particular, there are almost no systematic efforts in this field to compare and explain the differences among various Communist (and non-Communist) systems' [28].

There is certainly a daunting range of problems for empirical research and analysis: we must pose, as Feliks Gross recommends, three basic questions about any specific terrorist movement: for what? why? and against whom? ([52] p. 422). But of course we must range much further into problems of a comparative nature. Under what general political and socio-economic conditions do we find terrorism emerging? Can we account for varying patterns of terrorist ideology, organisation and practice? What are the conditions for their relative 'success' or 'failure'? Is it possible to make comparative assessments of the political and social effects of terrorism upon different types of political systems and social structure? What comparisons can we make concerning the impact of terrorist movements' tactics upon their popular appeal and support? How is popular support lost? How significant is the attitude of the population towards the terrorists in bringing 'success' to the latter? Does comparative analysis enable us to make any useful generalisations about the relative effectiveness of different counter-measures against terrorism? Last, but not least, is it possible to move forward from comparative analysis to useful theoretical models or theories of terrorism?

If one had to rely entirely upon data on contemporary active terrorist organisations, the difficulties of empirical research and comparative study might well seem too daunting to be worth attempting. Currently active terrorist movements do not encourage wide-eyed researchers to peer into their conspiracies and methods too closely. Their records have to be kept in the heads of their older, more experienced leaders or in private letters or diaries. Memories and papers will only tend to become accessible long after the fires of passion have subsided, when the cause has been 'lost' or 'won' or forgotten. Then the historian may have his chance to rake over the ashes – even then some may still be uncomfortably hot. With regard to the current operations of terrorists, discretion is the better part of valour for the researcher. Even the renegade who has a close knowledge of a particular terrorist organisation may be gambling with his own life if he compounds his schism by publication of full memoirs. It is a characteristic of terrorist movements that if they don't like the music they shoot the pianist. There are, of course, other major practical obstacles to the study of active, dormant and extinct terrorist movements. Like governments, much of their effort is directed towards psychological war, subversion and propaganda, and this means that much of terrorists' own publicity and political publication is at the very best unreliable, at worst a pack of lies.

Fortunately for the student of terrorism there is a wealth of individual historical studies which can provide invaluable material for comparative analysis and synthesis. Historical works have been drawn upon extensively for the present study as will be seen from the Bibliography. The historian's work serves to remind us that terrorism as a style of combat, as theory, ideology, organisation and practice has a history. Leaders and movements emulate each other. Histories of individual political terrorisms provide the raw material for comparison.

Before commencing with this task we must first attend to the immediate and pressing need to complete our business of concept formation and reconceptualisation. As Sartori and others have argued, we must try to construct more precise concepts with clear definitional attributes in order to facilitate orderly gathering and classification of information and a more discriminating analysis ([121] pp. 1033–53). The concept of political terrorism is far too all-embracing to be helpful as a tool for comparative politics. We must begin by setting out an elementary typology of the major varieties of political terrorism.

31

2. An Elementary Typology of Political Terrorism

We shall exclude from our typology *criminal terrorism* which can be defined as the systematic use of acts of terror for objectives of private material gain. Nor will the forms of purely *psychic terror* (religio-magical, etc.) be treated here. *War terrorism* will also be omitted on the grounds that a study of terroristic usages of war does not belong to an analysis of *political terrorism* proper. It might be objected that, in so far as wars are generally fought partly for political objectives, this is rather an arbitrary distinction. There is, indeed, such a reciprocal relationship between war and political terrorism that we shall find some reference to military events and developments unavoidable. On the other hand, phenomena of war or military terrorism have been quite inadequately studied and they really require separate and comprehensive treatment. There is, of course, a large literature on the so-called 'balance of terror', or what one authority has termed 'the relation of dual impotence between the two great powers armed with thermonuclear weapons' ([6] pp. 169 ff.). Yet remarkably little research has been undertaken into such tactics as the saturation bombing of cities or into alleged or admitted war crimes involving the massacre of civilians by military or naval forces. Is it even legitimate to describe such acts as terroristic if it can be shown that loss of life resulted only 'incidentally' in the course of realising purely military objectives (such as the destruction of enemy munitions, plants or communications)? Certainly each allegation of war terror needs to be studied in the light of all the available evidence concerning the initial military planning, the command structure, and the precise battle situation, in addition to the evidence of eyewitnesses. It would also be important and valuable in furthering our understanding of political terrorism to know more about the military effectiveness of war terror tactics aimed deliberately at undermining the morale of the civil population and weakening their will to resist. Is it the case, as Aron suggests, that such tactics will tend to be ultimately self-defeating, where the 'target population' is relatively homogeneous? Do such tactics serve only to make resistance more stubborn?

Several analysts of 'insurgency' and revolutionary terrorism have tried to clarify some fundamental distinctions between different forms of political terrorism. It is only fair to say that these attempts are rather parenthetical to their main preoccupation, which has generally been with the history and analysis of insurgent and counter-insurgent tactics. Crozier [27] distinguishes between *terror* as a weapon used by insurgents and *counter-terror*, by which he means the terror used against rebels by the government and its security forces, whose authority is being challenged. As Thornton has pointed out this is rather unsatisfactory because: 'It is by no means inevitable that the insurgents will initiate terrorism; in some instances, they may be reacting to the terror of the incumbents' ([136] p. 72). This seems a valid point as there is a clear implication that the 'counter-terrorists' did not start the terror. Thornton suggests, instead, the terms *enforcement terror* 'to describe terror launched by those in power' and *agitational terror* for 'terroristic acts by those aspiring to power' ([136] p. 72). Unfortunately this distinction will not provide an adequate basis for a typology, for several reasons. Neither 'enforcement' nor 'agitation' is a sufficiently comprehensive term to encompass the range of general aims which may motivate either incumbents or insurgents to employ terror. 'Enforcement' implies that power-holders use terror solely for the purpose of ensuring compliance to their decrees or orders among the population. In practice it has frequently been used for other purposes such as the liquidation of a scapegoat class or group. Certain states reserve the weapon of terror for counter-strikes against attacks by terrorist movements; it would be extremely misleading to confuse such objectives with enforcement. 'Agitational' is even less satisfactory. Individuals, factions or movements are rarely satisfied with the objective of shaking or disrupting the polity or creating agitation among the population at large. Historically, it is the case that many terroristic movements have had revolutionary aims. The ideologues and tacticians of such movements have been divided as to whether terror should be the major weapon in their struggle or whether it is really only a useful auxiliary. But, for the revolutionary, terror and popular agitation are not inevitably interlinked. For the revolutionary guerrilla force, terror is often regarded purely as an ancillary military technique to be used against the enemy's military forces. Debray, for example, accords it a role of limited value: 'Of course city terrorism cannot assume any decisive role, and it entails certain dangers of a political order. But if it is subordinate to the fundamental struggle (of the countryside), it has from the military point of view a strategic value; it immobilizes thousands of enemy soldiers in unrewarding tasks of protection' ([30] p. 74).

In Marxist–Leninist jargon the term 'agitation' refers to the special techniques of mobilising or influencing the masses by use of half-truths and emotive slogans. But in more general usage 'agitation' is a term which perhaps more accurately reflects the purposes of groups whose aims fall far short of revolution, but who may use terror tactics in order to achieve some passionately desired legislative reform or change of government policy. (An example is the use of bombs and arson by militant suffragettes, campaigning for votes for women.) Terror tactics may, of course, be adopted for a host of political motives other than revolution or agitation for reform. These include revenge against a particular official or group for a particularly hated decision, judgement, or policy; as a weapon in an inter-movement or intra-movement feud; as an act of partisan retaliation against an invasion of one's land or property, or against interference with one's customs, beliefs, or way of life; as a gesture in repudiation of the legitimacy of a regime.

A more thorough-going and valuable reconceptualisation is that of the sociologist, E. V. Walter [144, 145]. Walter has deployed his original conceptual framework with impressive skill in a comparative study of primitive regimes of terror which constitutes the first part of an ambitious projected comparative sociology of terror. He defines terrorism sociologically as the equivalent of a *process of terror* comprising 'the act or threat of violence, the emotional reaction, and the social effects'. Such processes are sustained by *systems of terror* which may or may not embrace a whole society or community. Where terror is confined to a special class or group within a society, as in a slave system, he defines this as a *zone of terror*. Walter distinguishes 'two major categories of systems of terror'. Firstly, there is the *siege of terror*, which is a system of terror directed at a revolutionary overthrow of the government or authority system and substituting rule either by the 'terror staff' or 'some other group approved by them' ([145] p. 7). The second is the *regime of terror* operated by power-holders. 'Instead of relying entirely on authority, conventional rules, and legitimate techniques, the men in power, for reasons to be discovered, choose to initiate the process of terror' ([145] p. 7). Now, whatever the merits of this sociological framework for the comparative study of primitive terror regimes, it falls disappointingly short of what is needed for the comparative analysis of political terrorism over the wide range of modern political systems. Walter concedes that terror may be resorted to by 'rebel groups' which lack the power to carry out a revolution. But, as we have already argued, this is only one of many conceivable motivations, falling short of revolution, which may inspire individuals or groups to undertake acts of terrorism. The term *regime of terror* may also add confusion for the political scientists for reasons which are fairly obvious. Regime is normally used in political studies to designate the governmental system of the state. Now, as Walter rightly emphasises, a system of terror may be restricted to a particular zone of society and implicitly its 'regime of terror' may in certain circumstances be confined to the zone of terror (e.g. slave-owners, or warders). Repressive terror is in many instances operated exclusively by specialist agencies or *apparats* of the state or by specific social groups (for example, many xenophobic movements and so-called 'vigilante' organisations). It is also the case that revolutionary movements can use terror to repress their own members or supposed supporters, just as revolutionary parties which are in power may use the agencies of government to promote revolutionary terror internally or abroad. It is necessary to construct a more flexible typology which is not rigidly tied to the ruler–ruled dichotomy and which encompasses terrorism which stems from motives other than revolution or repression. The outline for the following typology has already been sketched elsewhere [152].

Definition. Many movements and factions throughout history have resorted to *systematic tactics of terroristic violence with the objective of bringing about political revolution.* Those revolutionaries who succeed in gaining power often continue to use the revolutionary movement as a weapon of terror in order to maintain and carry through their revolutionary objectives and to destroy both real and imagined enemies.

Historical origin. Historians of the concept of revolution have rightly stressed that the idea of revolution originally had an entirely reactionary connotation [15, 79]. From Aristotle and Polybius to Machiavelli, it was considered part of the immutable cycle of human change, a mere turn in the wheel of fortune which threw one set of rulers to the dust only to raise others in their place. It was not until the eighteenth century that there clearly emerged ideas of revolutionary progress towards the realisation of a utopia of permanent freedom, happiness and material well-being. When the *philosophes* framed the conception of realising a heavenly kingdom on earth through rational human endeavour, they equipped politicians and popular leaders with a revolutionary ideology of potentially enormous power. The mid- and late-eighteenth century marks the beginnings of a European and ultimately world-wide diffusion of popular revolutionary ideology founded on the ideas of popular sovereignty and participation. But this magnetic new revolutionary ideology provided at the same time an ideological justification for *revolutionary terror.* No longer was extreme violence to be regarded, as hitherto, in terms of individual political ambition or the ruthless outcome of court or dynastic intrigue. Revolutionary terror is now seen as the just and lawful sanction of the people, violence sanctified in the name of the general will. The revolutionary Reign of Terror is thus in a real sense an invention of the French Revolution. Montesquieu had stressed the distinction between the republic based on the principle of 'virtu' and the dictatorship whose principle is 'fear'. In the period 1793–4 Robespierre and Saint-Just, as leaders of the revolutionary dictatorship, tried to reconcile these two principles. Saint-Just revealed himself as the archetypal revolutionary terrorist, however, because when he saw that appeal to republican virtue would fail to achieve his ends, he substituted terror alone.[12] However, it can be shown that the *organisation* and *method* of systematic terrorism were developed very much earlier in the course of sectarian conflict, notably by the Assassins in the Muslim world, from the late eleventh century onwards.

Attributes. It is essential for the process of precise reconceptualisation to define the essential attributes which distinguish revolutionary from other forms of terrorism. First, it is always a group, never a purely individual phenomenon, even though the size of the group involved may be very tiny. Second, there is invariably a revolutionary ideology or programme which is used to justify both the revolution and its terror: even a purely nihilistic or anarchistic ideology will serve this function in so far as it justifies the destruction of an existing order. The existence of leaders capable of mobilising people for terrorism is a third essential attribute. The importance of the factor of the availability of leaders has been stressed by theorists of collective behaviour in their theories of social movement [124]. This is, in the present writer's view, a more substantial and historically verifiable factor than the presence of certain personality types, which, as we shall observe later, is a related element stressed in some other theories ([46]; [52] pp. 466–9). A fourth attribute is that revolutionary terrorism creates alternative institutional structures. Peter Calvert correctly concludes that 'since these movements in some sense supplant the state by virtue of their very existence, they partake of the nature of the political system, and we may expect to find among anomic movements parallels to the regular institutions of organized government' ([15] p. 22). Many illustrations of these parallels are cited in our comparative analysis of revolutionary terrorism, and it can be shown that they develop their own policy-making executives, codes and 'law'.

Acquisition of weapons, however primitive, is a universal attribute of revolutionary terrorist movements, and allied to this is the necessity to acquire competence in terrorist methods

[12] On Saint-Just see Malraux [95] and Walter [146].

gained either by emulation or training. (This does not necessarily imply that they will always employ full-time professional terrorists.) One basic attribute is that revolutionary terrorists always attempt to keep their operational plans secret during both the preparatory and takeover phases of revolution. Unless terrorists are able to some extent to achieve this, their campaign will normally be aborted. Some writers lay great stress on the fact that some degree of popular support is necessary for the revolutionaries. (Normally, it is suggested that the sympathy of a sizeable minority, though not necessarily of a majority, is essential.) One could agree that this is certainly an important factor in accounting for the success of many revolutionary movements in seizing power. But we would not be justified in making a factor that properly belongs to a theory of revolution into a definitional attribute of revolutionary terrorism *sui generis*.

Sub-types. A number of sub-types of revolutionary terrorism can be usefully identified. Additional categories may suggest themselves to the reader. (i) Organisations of pure terror (in which terrorism is the exclusive weapon), (ii) revolutionary and national liberationist parties and movements in which terror is employed as an auxiliary weapon, (iii) guerrilla terrorism – rural and urban, (iv) insurrectionary terrorism – normally short-term terror in the course of a revolutionary rising, (v) the revolutionary Reign of Terror – often directed at classes and racial and religious minorities, (vi) propaganda of the deed, when this form of terror is motivated by long-term revolutionary objectives and (vii) international terrorism (that is terrorism committed outside the borders of one or all of the parties to the political conflict), when it is motivated by revolutionary objectives.

SUB-REVOLUTIONARY TERRORISM

Definition. Sub-revolutionary terrorism is employed *for political motives other than revolution or governmental repression*. Possible objectives include: attempts to compel governments to introduce a passionately desired policy or piece of legislation; revenge, or punishment, or warning against specific officials;

38

waging terror in a feud with rival factions or groups; retaliation against invasion of land or property, or against interference with a way of life.

Historical Origins. There is abundant historical evidence that this major type of terrorism is even older than revolutionary terrorism: assassination, 'sultanism', and dynastic assassinations have a very ancient history. We must be careful, however, to exclude tyrannicide from this category, as in cases where the justification for tyrannicide is very clear-cut we cannot confuse such acts with terrorism. Very real analytical difficulties do occur in the case of assassinations where the actual motivation of the assassin is unknown or uncertain. It is quite as dangerous to assume that every act of assassination must have a primarily political motive, as it is to assume the converse rule. It is often difficult to distinguish the ideologically militant individual terrorist from the psychopath 'whose shadowy voices prompt him to take his private revenge on society' ([65] p. 128). So many tragedies of individual terror transpire to be the work of pathetic publicity-seeking psychopaths, who apparently feel 'It's better to be wanted for murder than not to be wanted at all.'[13] Among the major historical determinants of sub-revolutionary terrorism have been: the existence of a tradition and culture of violence; the lack of any other accepted means for achieving political objectives within the societies concerned; or a long-standing history of feud. The feud is a generally intermittent series of acts of violence (usually including murder) committed by members of groups living within the same political frontiers or region. Feuding group members believe that they have a common obligation to avenge acts which they perceive as hostile or slighting committed by the rival group. Feuding groups take 'the law' into their own hands and refuse to leave matters of arbitration and sanction to the official legal system [12, 114].

Attributes. Sub-revolutionary terrorism is by nature even more highly unpredictable than other forms in terms of timing, targets and victims. Secondly, it is always extremely dangerous to the terrorist who in many instances acts alone without any

[13] The phrase derives from Marty Winch, *Psychology of the Wry* [154].

39

political or ideological supports. As in the case of revolutionary terrorism, operations must always be kept as secret as possible: indeed the need for secrecy is even greater in this type of action.

Sub-types. Vengeance, assassination, dynastic assassination, 'sultanism', feud (this may be strictly political or an expression of religious, class or race conflict), and partisan resistance terrorism are important sub-types. In general terms sub-revolutionary terrorism tends to have rather marginal political effects outside highly traditional autocracies in which the removal of the top man knocks the cornerstone out of the political structure. Nevertheless, both nationally and internationally, the containment and prevention of sub-revolutionary terrorism constitutes an increasingly serious problem. We shall be considering this problem in our discussion of counter-measures.

REPRESSIVE TERRORISM

Definition. Repressive terrorism is *the systematic use of terroristic acts of violence for the purposes of suppressing, putting down, quelling, or restraining certain groups, individuals or forms of behaviour* deemed to be undesirable by the repressor. The repressor may be the state, its rulers or agents, or a faction. It can be directed at the whole population or at selected groups. In the latter case it may confine the system of terror to what Walter terms specific 'zones of terror'. It may be mainly directed at insurgents or suspected insurgents (and this is sometimes misleadingly termed 'counter-terror'). Movements also frequently resort to repressive terrorism against their own members in order to coerce and control them.

Historical origins. Since the very earliest recorded history of human government, repressive terrorism has been the normal weapon of tyranny. Xenophon in *Tyrannicus* makes the tyrant, Hiero, admit that 'many tyrants have killed their own children', that tyrants proceed everywhere as through hostile territory, and are surrounded by enemies in their own cities. Suetonius, in *The Twelve Caesars*, gives a terrifyingly convincing picture of the conjunction of tyrannical power and madness suffered by

Rome in the reign of Nero. This notorious tyrant destroyed members of his own family, and the families of anyone who displeased him on the slightest whim. He engaged in a wholesale massacre of the nobility and wilfully set fire to the city ([132] VI, pp. 35–8).

The most explicit analysis of tyrannical methods of rule in the Renaissance is that provided by Machiavelli in *The Prince*. In his discussion of the 'villainous means' by which Agathocles the Sicilian and Oliverotto da Fermo took power, Machiavelli considers the reasons for their success in maintaining themselves in power after infinite treachery and cruelty. 'I believe this arises from the cruelties being exploited well or badly. Well-committed may be called those (if it is possible to use the word well of evil) which are perpetrated once for the need of securing one's self, and which afterwards are not persisted in, but are exchanged for measures as useful to the subjects as possible' ([87] VIII, p. 34). But here Machiavelli is allowing his own interest in prescribing for rationality and moderation to intervene. If a ruler, in seizing power, commits 'all his cruelties at once' but then proceeds to reassure the people and 'to win them over by benefiting them' then what we have is no longer tyranny but a form of benevolent despotism. It is essential to distinguish between tyrannical rule proper and caesarism, dictatorship and despotism, which may take both popular and benevolent forms. As Machiavelli notes in a different context: 'So to find a violent government joined with a good prince is impossible, because of necessity they become alike or one by the other is quickly destroyed. You must then believe either that you can hold this city with the utmost violence . . . or must be content with what authority we have freely given you' ([86] Book II, ch. 34). Now tyranny is rule by 'the utmost violence'. Tyrannical rule is characterised, as Walter remarks, by unconstitutional and illegitimate actions. Despotism may be defined 'as a system of arbitrary, unmediated power – adding the qualification that the power is legitimate' ([145] p. 55). It does not necessarily operate a system of terror though it may do so. Walter is, however, incorrect in asserting that Montesquieu misunderstands the fundamental principle of despotic government, for Montesquieu claims that this is not terror but *fear* and this is an important difference. 'Comme il faut de la vertu dans une république, et dans une monarchie, de'l'honneur, il faut de la CRAINTE dans un gouvernement despotique: pour la vertu, elle n'y est point nécessaire, et l'honneur y serait dangereux' ([102] III, 9). Some, though by no means all, despotisms institute repressive terror, but all despotism depends, in the last resort, upon fear of the ruler, obedience, and servility.

Attributes. Repressive terrorism is always arbitrary, unpredictable, and indiscriminate in its effects. Its perpetrators are not susceptible to the appeals of law or reason. Systematic repressive terror always becomes the responsibility of specialised agencies. No repressive state appears able to dispense with a secret police *apparat* whose members are specially trained in the methods of murder, torture, forced confessions, denunciation, subversion, etc. Such organisations have other tasks in addition to unthreading 'the bold eye of rebellion': hunting down all forms of political or even cultural dissent, imprisoning or liquidating those designated 'enemies' of the state or the revolution, spreading a network of informers into every corner of society, torturing and intimidating detainees to extract information, censorship, and the inculcation of conformity to the regime, for example by psychological warfare and 'brainwashing'. The terror *apparat* in the totalitarian regime is not initially deployed against Party members and political office holders. It is first directed against all political 'opposition', especially anarchists. Later whole peoples, ethnic groups, social classes, religious minorities, etc., may become its victims. Ultimately the terror is turned on the revolutionary followers themselves. It is not only the state which develops such terrorising agencies. The history of the Spanish Inquisition created such an instrument in the very bosom of the Church. Both the idea of the Inquisition and its methods of torture, informing, and extracting confessions were exploited and emulated by regimes throughout Europe. One authority on the medieval Church comments: 'Nothing could be more horrible reading than the record kept by the Spanish inquisitors of every word spoken by their victims under torture. Nothing can excuse such enormities. But a fair historical judgement should also take into consideration certain facts. The inquisitor believed an unrepentant heretic would go to hell, into that fire which Christ said "shall never be quenched": he tried by all means, short of torture itself if possible, to bring the heretic to confession. He hoped the heretic might repent even in the flames, and be saved "yet so as by fire" ' ([29] pp. 237–8). Not all torturers and executioners have had such high-minded purposes.

Sub-types. Systems of state terror, colonial terror, police terror, martial terror (where the state uses the army as a terror *apparat*), prison and prison-camp terror, slave terror, ideological and thought terror, and counter-insurgency terror, are all special forms of repressive terrorism.

Repressive terror does not receive any detailed comparative analysis in the present essay. Such a study is of course relevant and necessary, and there have been some interesting pioneer works in this field [4, 28, 104, 145]. Our preoccupation with the vast and complex range of sub-revolutionary and revolutionary terrorisms provides a daunting enough subject. The universe of revolutionary terrorisms is sufficiently large and varied for us to attempt some preliminary synthesis and generalisation. Readers should be aware of the invaluable histories of specific terrorist campaigns: these provide the essential material for such a venture, and the author's indebtedness to these sources is obvious from the Bibliography.

However, though it is important to bear in mind the ideological and intellectual antecedents and the many cases of emulation of terrorist theories and techniques, our aim has not been to produce a general history of terrorism. Our aim is analytic. Can we go beyond the essential task of identifying the features of terrorist theories, ideologies, organisations and tactics, and construct heuristically useful theories or models of revolutionary terrorism? Is it possible to relate the incidence, phasing and development of terrorism to a 'pathology' of political and socio-economic conditions, cultural *mores* or psychological and generational factors? Is terrorism passed on to new generations more by the unconscious influences of socialisation and tradition, or more through positive training and incitement to aggression and training in techniques of terrorist violence?

Another important range of questions concerns the relative effectiveness of terrorism as a political weapon. What are the basic conditions for its 'success' or 'failure', and how have these conditions been modified by new trends in terrorist tactics and patterns of governmental and societal response? Is the key to 'success' the winning of positive support from the majority of the population? Or is it enough to secure the neutrality or apathy of the majority while sustaining the militancy of the terrorist movement? Are there special dangers or costs of both a political and social-psychological nature which work to offset the apparent advantages of the terrorist weapon?

Last but by no means least we should examine some of the problems of (borrowing Leo Strauss's term) 'therapeutics'. Whether we find that certain kinds of political system are more susceptible and vulnerable to terrorism than others, or whether we conclude that they are all vulnerable in the long run, it will be helpful to compare the various anti-terrorist measures that have been either adopted or proposed by governments and international bodies. What counter-measures of both a short-term and a prophylactic nature are likely to be both practicable and effective?

3. Revolutionary and Sub-revolutionary Terrorism

A. THE RIGHTEOUS ASSASSINS

Murder for motives of political ambition and rivalry was well known to the ancients, as the classical histories bear witness. Sennacharib was murdered by his two sons. Many Roman emperors murdered their rivals and even decimated their own families. The actual motives of tyrants such as Tiberius and Nero are as hard to speculate about as those of Stalin, but clearly madness, jealousy and hatred, as well as sheer lust for power, were involved. Thus the mad Caligula arranged the murder of Tiberius in order to clear the path for his own accession. Some of these murders were inspired by paranoid suspicion, others were provoked by fear of an evil augury. Yet whatever the pretext, none of these murders, with the sole exception of tyrannicide, was given explicit religious or ideological justification. Though often associated with *coups* or Praetorian conspiracies they were not committed in the name of popular revolutionary ideology or religious legitimacy. As Feliks Gross observes, 'At the time of the Emperor Constantine, it became a method later called "sultanism", a continuous murder of all possible pretenders to power, or competitors, until no one but the ultimate ruler survived' ([52] p. 423).

Perhaps the first organised group systematically employing murder for a cause it believed to be righteous was the famous Muslim sect, the Assassins, from whose name the modern word 'assassination' derives. Early Christian travellers and the Crusaders encountered members of this sect in Syria and an enormous web of legend and fantasy was woven around their experiences. It is only fairly recently that European historians have been able to reappraise these earlier accounts in the light of the general development of Islamic history and to distinguish the crucial facts about the sect from the colourful embellishments of medieval romances. The sect belonged to a larger dissident sect, the Ismailis, who were part of the Shiá, one of the two major warring factions of Islam. Some of the Ismaili sect's followers formed a powerful base in Persia while another branch, the Khojas, were to be found in India. The name 'Assassin' almost certainly derives from the Syrian word *hashishi*. Hashish came to denote the narcotic cannabis, and some scholars have suggested that the Assassins must have been addicts. A modern authority considers that the Syrian word signifies contempt for the bizarre nature of the sectaries' beliefs and behaviour, rather than a literal description of their habits [81]. The real interest for the student of terrorism lies in the fact that they developed an explicit religious justification for killing the unrighteous and the servants of the unrighteous. There is some support in early Islamic doctrine for the principles of tyrannicide and just rebellion and the Assassin doctrines re-emphasised these obligations, but, in addition, we should note that each act of murder was for the Assassin a *sacramental duty*. The weapon used was invariably a dagger. This made the apprehension of the Assassin all the more likely. Moreover there is evidence that sectaries willingly sacrificed their own lives. We are dealing here with the phenomenon of fanatical believers who killed because they believed themselves to be righteous and because they believed that killing the unrighteous would guarantee their own salvation and assist in overthrowing a corrupt order.

The Assassins formed a tight-knit disciplined brotherhood, inspired by the teachings of Hasan-i Sabbah. From the end of the eleventh century they began to pit a new weapon against their religious and political opponents, the Seljuq military forces and Sunni Islam. Instead of the previous hopeless attempts at insurrection they perfected techniques of systematic terrorism which certainly wrought terror not only among the Muslim potentates and chiefs (whose personal style of rule made them extremely vulnerable to the Assassins), but even among Christian princes who had been regaled by tales of the Assassins' stealth and fanaticism. The Assassin's Master was known as The Old Man of the Mountain and they were as blindly obedient to him as they were to their sacrificial faith in the New

Preaching of Ismaili religion. Two of their organisational practices have an extraordinarily modern ring. First was their emphasis on popular agitation, the energetic attempt to spread their beliefs among the townspeople and the peasants. Of course we must remember that they were working not as political ideologues but as *missionaries* spreading a new religious teaching. They also applied the strict code of secrecy among all members of the organisation, a feature which is vital in the creation and sustaining of any terrorist movement. In the manner of later terrorists they were frequently able to terrorise local political authorities into compromise or even into active co-operation with them, and in true guerrilla fashion they sought secure bases for retreat, seizing control of certain especially remote areas and capturing fortresses. Sometimes rulers in major cities would exploit alliance with the Assassins for their own advantage. Their terror was directed against key individual representatives of the Sunni Muslim order, its religious and political leaders and princes, and was often symbolic or propagandist in intent and sometimes directed at the highest levels of the Seljuq structure (for example, the murder of several Caliphs).

Whence came their support? Lewis argues that it was certainly not, except during the period of the New Preaching, a powerful intellectual appeal. He suggests rather that the Assassins were a multi-class coalition including a few from the families of notables, dedicated to a fundamentally millenarian fanaticism. In view of the rather scanty evidence on the social origins and objectives of the sect we would perhaps be wise to be somewhat sceptical of those rival theories of the Assassins which tend to see the movement through contemporary ideological lenses. Some have argued that it was a popular movement of the poor against the Seljuq order. Gobineau believed it to have been an early expression of nationalism in Persia. Another interpretation holds that the Assassins mark a phase in the rearguard defensive action of the feudal lords against the forces of centralisation and urbanisation. The Assassins were ultimately unsuccessful in their objective of destroying the Sunni orthodoxy. Nevertheless, they were, by virtue of their beliefs, tactics and form of organisation, the prototypal terrorist movement [81].

Western and central European rulers did not, of course, need any external example or influence to encourage them to resort readily and with increasing frequency to the expediences of political murder which characterised the Renaissance states. We have already noted that the practice known as 'sultanism' was well established in Rome and did not have to be imported through cultural contact with the expanding Muslim empire. Moreover, the doctrinal tensions, conflicts and schisms of Christendom itself provided the bases for early religio-ideological justifications: the legitimacy of elective and consecrated rulers could already be put in serious question if doubt could be cast upon their piety and religious obedience. As early as the fifth century A.D. Christian theologians made a distinction between cities or states where the ruler's sovereignty was founded purely on *force majeure* and those sovereignties based upon some degree of justice and legitimacy:

> In the absence of justice, what is sovereignty but organized brigandage? For what are bands of brigands but petty kingdoms? They also are groups of men, under the rule of a leader, bound together by a common agreement, dividing their booty according to a settled principle. If this band of criminals, by recruiting more criminals, acquires enough power to occupy regions, to capture cities, and to subdue whole populations, then it can with fuller right assume the title of kingdom, which in the public estimation is conferred upon it, not by the renunciation of greed, but by the increase of impunity ([7] Book IV, p. 4).

There had developed, by the High Middle Ages, a fully articulated Christian doctrine for the justification of individual acts of tyrannicide to save the Christian commonwealth from evil rule. More significant still for the history of Renaissance and Reformation Europe was the emergence of a more explicit doctrine of just rebellion. Both the work of Thomist philosophers, and writings of more radical thinkers such as Marsilio of Padua's *In Defensor Pacis*, began to provide more powerful justifications for the overthrow of rulers who defied the laws of God, that is to say those who went against natural and moral law. It was a short step from using such doctrines to sanction war against the rule of unbelievers (such as the Saracens) to invoking them against excommunicates and any prince who would be deemed an apostate. Now such religio-ideological justifications were widely resorted to in individual conflicts between popes and emperors, princes and prelates well before the period of the Great Schism. They became the usual means of justifying the murders of political and religious opponents which became the stock-in-trade of Renaissance monarchies. Nevertheless, in both theory and practice, the medieval concepts of legitimacy based on hereditary succession, election and consecration by the Church remained free from any fundamental challenge until the Reformation. The most serious inroads against it were made in the Italian Renaissance states where the sultanist traditions of palace revolution and dynastic assassination took firm root. They called forth a new political science of shameless expediency entirely divorced from considerations of any higher moral law, explored most candidly in the writings of Machiavelli. But despite this break with the norms of medieval morality and legitimacy there was as yet no appeal to a purely political ideology of popular revolution. If there was any rationalisation provided for overturning a throne it was generally based on either the grounds of 'defence of true religion' or a counter-claim to hereditary right.

It is not until the French revolutionary period that the political–ideological basis is created to provide an entirely secular justification for revolution in the name of the popular will. A revolutionary theory of popular rights to liberty and justice provides the first powerful ideological justification for revolutionary terrorism proper, a terror that was in the eyes of the ideologues of the Revolution a legitimate weapon of revolutionary justice and revenge against the absolutist, aristocratic and ecclesiastical systems of the *ancien régime*. Revolutionary terror was the child of the French Revolution and its first directors were men like Robespierre, Marat, Saint-Just, and Fouché.

There is a passage which bitterly conveys the paradox of the revolutionary terror in Peter Weiss's *Marat/Sade* when Corday flings at Marat:

'Once both of us saw the world must go
and change as we read in great Rousseau
but change meant one thing to you I see
and something quite different to me
The very same words we both have said
to give our ideals wings to spread
      but my way was true
      while for you
the highway led over mountains of dead' ([150] p. 14).

The highway of the Terror on the most authoritative estimates certainly cost thousands of lives: Greer suggests approximately 40 000 deaths and roughly 300 000 arrests [50, 78].

The historians of the French Revolution are largely agreed that in its initial phase incidents of terroristic violence were infrequent but spontaneous acts of insurrectionary mob vengeance and class hatred against aristocrats rather than the result of a systematic policy. The gruesome public tortures and executions were but one expression of this and attacks on the property of the Church and nobility were often the occasion for mass terror. The famous street ballad *Ça Ira* was a boast of vengeance:

> Long live the sound of cannons
> Ah ça ira
> To the lantern with the aristocrats
> Ah ça ira
> We're going to string up the aristocrats[14]

There were occasions of mass terror in 1792: the storming of the Tuileries in August and the September Massacres, when it is estimated that about one-half of the Paris prison population was massacred ([78] p. 230). Apart from these terrible events there was no widespread indiscriminate slaughter in the early phase of the Revolution.

The idea of a *policy* of revolutionary terror originated with the Jacobins. Robespierre, Saint-Just, and the Committee of Public Safety all influenced, to some extent, the first wholesale attempt

[14] Written in 1792, translated by Clive Emsley. The third verse is quoted by Mervyn Williams ([153] p. 102).

to implement it from 1793 to 1794. It is clear that Robespierre had his hand forced on the issue of terror. The Hébertists and the Jacobin Club had been clamouring that 'terror be made the order of the day'. What decided the matter after the summer of 1793 was the worsening of the war threat to the survival of the revolutionary regime, a threat which had been building up since the outbreak of the War of Coalition in April 1792. The war threat against a France already racked by internal conflict with the counter-revolutionary forces and by schisms among the revolutionaries simply intensified the fear of subversion and the climate of mutual suspicion and denunciation. One authority notes,

> Inevitably, war gave a fresh encouragement to those seeking to destroy the Revolution from within and without and provoked, in turn, exceptional measures against counter-revolution, aristocracy and 'fanaticism'. . . . Through inflation, treachery, defeat and social disturbance, it compelled the Assembly, contrary to its own cherished principles, to set up a strong 'revolutionary' government, to institute the Terror, to control prices and to mobilize the nation for war ([119] p. 124).

It certainly is clear that Robespierre saw there were serious political risks involved. Terror could so easily be turned from 'public enemies' against the people itself.

What of the organisation and direction of the Reign of Terror which lasted from the summer of 1793 to the summer of 1794? Its vital instrument was the Law of Suspects, passed on 17 September 1793, which literally enabled the Committee of General Security and the Revolutionary Tribunal to round up anyone they liked on the merest suspicion of treachery. A much-hated development was the recruitment of a veritable army of informers linked to the national police system. Saint-Just was a great believer in perfecting the system of informers and believed in using the Terror to control every sector of life: 'Dans son système, quiconque ne dénoncait pas était complice . . .' ([95] p. 121). In late 1793 the Jacobins created special Representatives-on-Mission to carry the Terror into the provinces, men like Fouché the 'Executioner' of Lyons and Javogues in the Loire. These operated with terrible effect. On occasion they employed special detachments of the Armée Révolutionnaire of Paris to round up suspects who were then summarily executed. At Lyons a special form of mass execution was used by the Revolutionary Army. Victims were chained together and shot at by cannon loaded with grapeshot. Any who survived the cannonade were immediately shot down by rifle-fire. A mass grave of quicklime was prepared in advance. Some accounts of the work of the Representatives-on-Mission imply that they enjoyed considerable freedom of action, indeed more autonomy than Paris wished or intended. Fouché protested in his own defence that he was simply 'acting under the strict orders of the Committees of General Security and Public Safety'.[15] Lucas has provided an excellent study of Javogues and the Terror in the Loire [85].

There were other barbarous methods of execution, such as mass-drowning, employed in this phase of the Revolution in addition to the *mitraillades* and the guillotine. It does seem clear, however, that the worst excesses of the Representatives-on-Mission and the Armée Révolutionnaire took place precisely in those regions where counter-revolutionary resistance had been most stubborn. Moreover, they were also balanced by the atrocities of the counter-revolutionaries in areas such as the Vendée. Yet the major innovation of the Reign of Terror was, as Richard Cobb argues, the elaboration of a method of *preventive revolutionary repression* from the Law of Suspects onwards. It was based on the generalisation of *suspicion* not simply against individuals, but against whole classes, groups or parties who were designated *potential* enemies of the revolution. As Cobb remarks: 'This method, which Fouché claims with some justification to have truly invented, showed itself to be extraordinarily effective in the course of the next 150 years' ([20] p. 207).

The other innovation of the French revolutionaries of major significance in the history of terrorism was the *ideological terror*, which had as its inevitable corollary the periodic attempts to

[15] See Fouché's own account in *Memoires de Joseph Fouché, duc d'Otrante*, edités et rédigés en partie par Alphonse de Beauchamp, vol. 1 (Paris: Le Rouge, 1824) pp. 44 ff.

control thought, art, literature and the press by the devices of terror, intimidation and censorship. It found its fullest expression when the latent anti-clericalism of the early phases of the Revolution was whipped up into a full-scale 'dechristianisation' campaign in the Terror of 1793–4. Representatives-on-Mission, such as Collot d'Herbois and Fouché, were responsible for directing seizures of churches, confiscation of church plate and valuables and the demolishing of religious statues. Often the Revolutionary Army detachments joined in with local anti-clerical societies in special ceremonies to mock and revile the Pope, priests and all believers. Many priests were slaughtered in the Terror. Some, of course, did collaborate with the terrorists, donning the red Cap of Liberty, and joining in celebration of the 'Feast of Reason'. But, especially in provinces where royalist resistance had been very strong, the priests were automatically regarded as enemies of the Revolution. Over a hundred were killed in the mass executions at Lyons, and at Nantes many were killed by drowning in the Loire. Many more languished in the terrible dungeons inherited from the *ancien régime*. The majority of victims of the ideological terror were not traitors, and no truly impartial tribunal could have convicted them of any crime. They were victims of a terror which confused all deviationists with the enemy. Some ideologues have frankly admitted as much: 'A patriot is one who supports the Republic as a whole; whoever resists it in detail is a traitor' (Saint-Just); 'In reality the most serious threat to civilization is not to kill a man because of his ideas (this has often been done in wartime), but to do so without recognizing it or saying so, and to hide revolutionary justice behind the mask of the penal code' (Merleau-Ponty).

What does this admission amount to? Surely nothing more or less than the claim that revolutionary justice amounts to the mere will or whim of the revolutionary terrorist. The revolutionary Reign of Terror in France therefore marks a watershed in the transition from the individual executions planned by the righteous Assassins, and of those attempting tyrannicide, to the revolutionary terrorist executing in the name of the collective good of the people as rationalised in terms of the political ideology of the prevailing revolutionary leadership.

Thus we wish to argue that the essential characteristics of revolutionary terrorism emerged not in the late nineteenth century as many earlier writers on terrorism have contended, but with the Jacobins.

Many of the purely organisational characteristics of revolutionaries' conspiratorial secret societies can be traced back to even earlier origins. We have already noted the example of the tight discipline, rule of obedience and strict secrecy practised by the Ismaili sectaries. In the Occident we can trace such organisational models much earlier than the Illuminati, the Freemasons, and the host of revolutionary secret societies of the eighteenth century which have been the subject of several studies [58, 88]. Coser has drawn attention to the close *organisational* similarity between the early Society of Jesus and the early Bolshevik Party [24]. He defines both phenomena as belonging to the 'militant collective' organisational type. Both required a *total* dedication to the service and objectives of the organisation on the part of the individual initiate. There were no 'members' in the usual sense, only full-time professional agents or soldiers. Kinship ties and other cross-cutting loyalties were strongly discouraged by the organisation. Members were cut off from all local roots as far as possible so that, like soldiers, they could be ready to serve anywhere at a moment's notice. Blind obedience to commands of superiors was inculcated. This para-military command structure is certainly a feature common to most terrorist organisations. On the other hand the strict asceticism which was demanded of the model Jesuit is not generally demanded of the personal lives of most political terrorists. It is indeed somewhat doubtful whether it was a feature of the early Bolshevik Party organisation. The Party had to come before everything. That went without saying. But what you did in your sexual and personal relationships was considered irrelevant to the cause of the Revolution unless your hobby happened to be informing to the Okhrana. It would be misleading to push such organisational analogies too far, however, despite the wealth of evidence concerning certain points of similarity. The differences between terrorist and other forms of religious and ideological movement are crucial. Terrorist movements instil their members with the belief that *any means* may be justified for the ends of the movement. Whole groups as well as individuals may be deemed expendable and must be eliminated by any terrorist on the order of the movement. Their forms of oath-taking for initiates, their rules of obedience, all bind the member ever more tightly to the brotherhood through deepening involvement, both individual and collective, in systematic political murder.

As Stavrogin explains to Verkhovensky in a famous passage in *The Possessed*:

'Can you count on your fingers the people who can be accepted as members of your circles? All this is just bureaucracy and sentimentality – all this is just so much cement, but there's one thing that is much better: persuade four members of the circle to murder a fifth on the excuse that he is an informer and you'll at once tie them all up in one knot by the blood they've shed. They'll be your slaves' ([33]] p. 388).

Dostoyevsky saw all too clearly that terrorist societies devour their own members. Terror becomes the accepted weapon for both helping to maintain obedience, secrecy and loyalty, and as the ultimate sanction against the deviant member. In making a distinction between what he calls the *survival group* and the *pledged group*, Sartre makes the additional point that, in the case of the pledged group in which 'nothing material binds the members', a sense of danger, fear and anxiety has to be reinvented to hold the group together when no obvious external threat exists. Thus terrorism becomes 'the reign in the group of absolute violence on its members' [76].

B. TERROR AGAINST INDIGENOUS AUTOCRACY

Until the French Revolution the response of rebels against the repression of autocracy was generally limited to individual assassination attempts, armed self-defence and riot. It was the Jacobins who developed the idea of pitting the utmost violence of the revolutionaries against the forces of traditionalism and autocracy. When Saint-Just set up his revolutionary commission at Strasbourg he declared, 'Les prévaricateurs des administrations seront fusillés' ([95] p. 123). This was the authentic voice of revolutionary terror. Yet it could only be brought into full play when the autocracy of the *ancien régime* had been overthrown and the major political obstacles to revolutionary terror removed. What lessons could those rebels who lived under the deadweight of well-entrenched absolutisms elsewhere in Europe, especially Russia and the Balkans, draw from events in the West? In Russia, for example, there was no real tradition of urban revolutionary insurrection, although there were, according to the estimate of the Russian historian Semevsky, over 500 peasant insurrections in Russia between 1800 and 1861. The main critics of the tsars' autocratic government, the liberal intelligentsia, constituted a tiny island of western cultural influences in a sea of slav feudalism. Some caught hold eagerly of French revolutionary ideas of popular insurrection as the essential strategy for a popular, egalitarian revolution. Such ideas had been fostered by Babeuf and the Conspiracy of Equals between 1794 and 1796. Babeuf in turn influenced Buonarotti and Auguste Blanqui, and Blanquist followers both in France and Russia developed plans for a series of co-ordinated armed insurrections to be led by an elite vanguard trained in revolutionary combat. Yet though the Blanquists in France and Russia clearly espoused a strategy of armed violence, this was not seen as necessitating terrorist tactics. Despite the abysmal failure of the Decembrist revolt in Russia (1825) and the evident impotence of the Russian Blanquists, it was not until the 1870s that terrorism became clearly established as the major weapon of several revolutionary groupings in Russia. Before examining the development of terrorism in Russia we suggest some general observations on autocracies.

The majority of both recent and contemporary governments have been autocracies of one kind or another. It is useful for comparative purposes to subdivide them into traditional and modernising types, though it must be noted that programmes of social and economic modernisation are not necessarily accompanied by programmes of political development aimed at a transition to democratic government. Some, of course, may be attracted towards emulating the totalitarian model. In comparing autocracies we must take into account socio-economic

56

and cultural data such as rates of economic growth, population growth and literacy rates, and the important political variables which include (i) the degree of legitimacy achieved by the regime, (ii) its degree of internal stability, (iii) the presence or absence of a tradition of political violence within the political culture, (iv) the capabilities and effectiveness of the regime's military and security forces, (v) the degree to which the regime is constrained by constitutional or judicial considerations such as the claim to recognise certain basic individual rights, (vi) the readiness of rebels to accept encouragement, aid and guidance from abroad, (vii) the quantity and quality of military weaponry and personnel available to the rebels from whatever source, (viii) the availability of a justifying ideology for the use of terrorism among the rebels, and a knowledge of terrorist techniques.

Autocracies of imperialist or colonialist type are considered in the next section; they are of far less importance currently, but they were, in the recent past, the major targets of revolutionary terrorism. Inevitably for the colonial inhabitants or for those subjected to the rule of an alien conqueror, the oppression or injustice implicit in autocratic government is compounded by hatred of foreign rule. There are some surviving colonial regimes (for example, enclaves in Africa, Asia and the Pacific) but the overwhelming majority of present-day autocracies are indigenous. Even so, many autocracies contain irredentist minorities who may continue to regard the 'native' autocracy as alien and where this separatist feeling combines with other grievances concerning unequal treatment, oppression, or deprivation, the possibilities of terrorist revolutionary movements emerging are enhanced. For example, the Russian anarchist movement *Chernoe Znamia* (Black Banner), which was the first of many anarchist groups to wage deliberate systematic terror in Russia in the early 1900s, contained many Ukrainian, Polish and Jewish members, and Avrich [8] has emphasised that they gained their largest following in the southern and western frontier provinces.

The evidence for regarding the transitional states in the process of rapid modernisation as those most prone to political instability and acute civil violence has been cogently presented by Huntington [62]. Many writers have stressed the importance of relative deprivation (perceived expectations outstripping available resources) and the sudden blocking of progress for a group that has experienced a marked increase in income, status or power (the so-called J-curve effect). The Feierabend and Nesvold comparative data on the frequency of assassinations (1948–67) contained in Table 1 show that indicators of civil violence in general may not be equally applicable to assassination and terror. All but two of the twelve highest-scoring states are certainly 'transitional' by Huntington's criteria. Yet we must also reckon with the awkward fact that the United States, France, and Japan, all highly developed industrialised constitutional democracies, figure among the fifteen states with the highest number of assassinations out of a total of eighty-four investigated for that period.

If we survey the politics of Latin America, where autocratic modernising states are the norm, we certainly find abundant evidence of civil violence in the form of *coups*, violent demonstrations, and political murders and, of course, a high incidence of repressive terror. Latin America has seen some of the worst examples of repressive terrorist regimes, for example, in Haiti (both under the 'Doc' Duvalier regime and its successor), in Brazil, and in Batista's Cuba. Yet, as we shall have reason to observe, terrorism has not in general been adopted as a main weapon of revolutionary movements in the region, with the outstanding exception of the Tupamaros in Uruguay, where it has been employed against one of the most constitutionally liberal and welfare-minded of all Latin-American governments! Clearly, therefore, in order to explain relatively rare cases of revolutionary movements adopting terrorism against indigenous autocracy we need to take into account certain political factors already noted above, such as the special cultural or ideological conditions which may be conducive to terrorism, the role of the revolutionary leadership, and the presence or absence of effective governmental response. Hence we cannot equate the preconditions for terrorism with a general support for revolution *per se*. Paradoxically, in those countries where the desire to be rid of a regime may be strongest, the chances for any revolutionary opposition (whether terrorist or not) even gaining a

Table 1

Frequencies of Assassinations, 1948–67

Country	Number of Assassinations	Country	Number of Assassinations
Bulgaria	0	Israel	3
Chile	0	Italy	3
China (Taiwan)	0	Mexico	3
Denmark	0	Paraguay	3
East Germany	0	Republic of South Africa	3
Finland	0	Thailand	3
Honduras	0	Turkey	4
Iceland	0	Burma	5
Ireland (Eire)	0	Cyprus	5
Luxembourg	0	Czechoslovakia	5
Netherlands	0	Greece	5
Norway	0	Haiti	5
Peru	0	Indonesia	5
Poland	0	Iraq	5
Romania	0	Nicaragua	5
Sweden	0	Pakistan	5
Switzerland	0	Panama	5
United Kingdom	0	Cambodia	6
Uruguay	0	Jordan	6
U.S.S.R.	0	Malaya	6
Austria	1	Colombia	7
Belgium	1	Dominican Republic	7
Canada	1	Ghana	7
Hungary	1	Syria	7
Libya	1	India	8
New Zealand	1	Argentina	9
Sudan	1	Bolivia	9
Afghanistan	2	Japan	9
Albania	2	Laos	10
Australia	2	Brazil	12
Ceylon	2	Guatemala	12
Costa Rica	2	Lebanon	12
El Salvador	2	Venezuela	12
Ethiopia	2	Egypt	14
Liberia	2	France	14
Portugal	2	Philippines	15
Saudi Arabia	2	Tunisia	16
Spain	2	United States	16
West Germany	2	Morocco	17
Yugoslavia	2	Iran	19
China (Mainland)	3	Korea	20
Ecuador	3	Cuba	28

Source: from I. K. and R. Feierabend and Betty A. Nesvold, 'The Comparative Study of Revolution and Violence' [39] p. 395. Note that a table for the period since 1968 would show a high U.K. frequency because of the Northern Ireland assassinations.

foot-hold may be remote. In examining an archetypal case of terrorism against autocracy – the Russian experience – we find that the development of a critical intelligentsia and a discussion of alternative revolutionary strategies and tactics were facilitated to a large extent by the regime's introduction of a limited measure of freedom of expression as well as by the dashing of earlier hopes for genuine progress towards a popular democracy. We must now consider some of the alternative theories of revolution and reform which were influential among the Russian intelligentsia, and in particular those ideas which favoured terrorism, the ideologies used to justify it, the development and deployment of its tactics and techniques, and the consequences of terrorism for Russia.

Revolutionaries in nineteenth-century Russia confronted what was arguably the most reactionary and oppressive autocracy in nineteenth-century Europe. At the base of the social pyramid was the vast majority, the peasant population, whose legal status until the emancipation of 1861 was feudal serfdom. Interposed between the peasant masses and the nascent and relatively powerless bourgeoisie was the new class of urban workers, and above the bourgeoisie came the church, the army and the nobility, the three crucial supports for the tsar's personal autocracy, the apex of the structure. The tsar was not only ruler over all the Russian empire, he was also seen as Father of the People and as the Divinely-appointed head of the Russian Orthodox Church, as well as secular ruler. While the tsar, the court, and the wealthy nobility lived a life of ostentatious luxury, serfs were treated as a sub-human form of life and regarded as ineligible for rights of citizenship and as being only fitted to do menial work and to live in degrading squalor. When the peasants rose in desperation against their masters which, as we have noted, happened frequently in the nineteenth century, they were beaten down by repressive measures of barbaric cruelty. All political agitation among them was outlawed and indeed all discussion of possible social and political reforms was almost inevitably regarded as potentially revolutionary by the tsars and their ministers.

Like all modern autocracies, Russia did not prove to be immune against pressures for social change, both internally and

60

externally induced. It was impossible to keep out all the liberalising ideas and influences of the West. The requirement for new skills and higher levels of education led the Russian regime to develop public education. By the end of Alexander I's reign (1825) 6 universities, 48 state secondary schools and 337 improved state primary schools had been established. These helped to create a powerful engine for the destruction of the feudal autocracy – the small but influential radical intelligentsia. This intelligentsia, as historians of modern Russia agree, did not have a monolithic class composition. It contained many of aristocratic birth, but also elements from the petty bourgeoisie (though these tended to be a rather isolated sub-group) and, increasingly from the 1850s onwards, it gained support from the *raznochintsy* (those of working-class or peasant origins) ([111] p. 407; [155] pp. 45–51). Its members tended to be concentrated around the university centres, particularly St Petersburg and Moscow, and the student bodies of the universities and institutes were its vital sources of recruitment. In a regime where any political agitation is regarded with suspicion the intelligentsia becomes identified in the minds of the authorities with radicalism and revolt. But it is important to recognise how isolated and vulnerable such a group can be in a rigidly hierarchical and authoritarian social structure. The bulk of the nobility remained suspiciously aloof from the intelligentsia, and looked anxiously to the government to protect them against incipient peasant revolt, to help service their accumulating debts, and to maintain their privileges. The bourgeoisie was small and effectively without political power, while the outlook of the peasantry had its own esoteric qualities. Peasants could not sympathise with bourgeois concern over the protection of individual property rights: they tended to cherish hopes of a simple peasant communism based on the life of the *mir*, and to distrust townsmen of all classes. Periodic famine, chronic land-hunger and callous or unjust treatment at the hands of their masters, all the standing grievances of the peasantry, were not adequately redressed by the Emancipation of 1861 and the succeeding land reforms. Indeed, a new spate of riots ensued in the 1860s in protest against both the inadequacy of the individual land-holdings made available to peasants and against the payments of redemption dues demanded from them.

Already in the mid-nineteenth century, the tiny radical intelligentsia was beginning to identify 'The Cause' as the achievement of social justice for the Russian peasantry. Indeed the predominant ideological strand among the radical intelligentsia in nineteenth-century Russia was not anarchist or Blanquist but rather populist and Russophil. Even intellectual leaders such as Alexander Herzen and Nikolai Ogarev, who were well aware of western liberal thought and influences, tended to romanticise and idealise the Russian peasantry and to envisage their emancipation as the means of general emancipation of Russian society. In their journal *Kolokol* (*The Bell*) they argued that peasant collectives could become the basis of a new Russian socialism, and claimed western European models of parliamentary democracy to be potentially corrupting and irrelevant to Russia's needs. But how were the populists to achieve their new socialist society? Their intellectual leaders found it even more difficult to agree on the right means, than to identify long-term objectives.

The first significant step towards a permanent populist terror organisation is the establishment of *Zemlya Volya* (Society of Land and Liberty) in 1876, through the efforts of Alexander Mihailov, Mark Natanson and Aron Zundelevich. For the first time they formed a specialist terror group under their Administrative Centre with the tasks of liquidating traitors and police spies and to release comrades from prison. Land and Liberty first became involved in assassination when one of their number, Vera Zasulich, privately decided to avenge the brutal flogging of a comrade, Bogolyubov, by shooting General Trepov (Governor-General of St Petersburg) who had ordered the flogging. Zasulich's shot did not kill Trepov, but it did much to publicise the existence of the revolutionary movement and to encourage them to further exploits. Land and Liberty was by no means unanimous, however, regarding the desirability of terrorist methods. In 1879 the movement split; the Black Partition section, who favoured economic and social action, later followed Plekhanov into the Social Democrats. The pro-terrorist group took the name *Narodnaya Volya* (People's Will) and Zhelyabov and Mikhailov were among its leading organisers. It was this group which succeeded in assassinating Tsar Alexander II in 1881, using a team of bomb throwers. A child bystander was killed by one of the bombs. There was an element of revenge in the declared motives of the assassins: their statement declared that the tsar had been killed because, among other crimes, he had hanged or exiled anyone who resisted on behalf of the people or in the cause of justice.

It is perhaps not really surprising that the government responded by a campaign of bitter repression. It is fairly clear that Alexander III was already thoroughly inculcated with the uncompromisingly autocratic doctrines of his tutor, Pobedonostsev. The more moderate reformist ideas of Loris-Melikov (adviser to Alexander II), who wished to deprive *Narodnaya Volya* of any popular support by a programme of popular reform, were doomed under the new leadership. A manifesto of May 1881 actually proclaimed that Alexander III would uphold autocracy 'with faith in the power and right of autocracy', and Pobedonostsev stubbornly opposed any move towards representative democracy, a free press or free elections. He even used the Orthodox priests to augment the secret police system by using them as informers. The government brought in the notorious 'Temporary Regulations' which empowered them to make summary arrests and to bring suspects before court-martial. With the accompanying expansion of secret police activity and the increasingly sophisticated use of police informers infiltrating the revolutionary movement, *Narodnaya Volya* was almost, but not quite, forced out of existence. Its leading champion, Vera Figner, was forced to move out of St Petersburg to cities where the police were less well organised, first to Moscow, then to southern Russia. Funds dwindled to a trickle. New cells were speedily tracked down and extinguished. But Figner and others did keep alive the belief in the indispensability and efficacy of terrorist tactics, and a knowledgeable experience of terrorist techniques, which were transmitted to new generations of terrorist recruits.

Populist terrorism reached the zenith of its popularity as a revolutionary method in Russia under the Social-Revolutionaries. This party had been formed in the 1890s in rivalry with Plekhanov and Axelrod's Social Democrats. Its members were largely recruited from the old guard of *Narodnaya Volya* and its younger sympathisers, and its major objective was to bring about a social revolution which would give all land to the peasants and establish an agrarian socialist Russia. They quickly established (in autumn 1901) a specialist terrorist section called the Battle Organisation which was to become the predominant force in the Party, and its first major 'success' was the assassination of the Minister of the Interior, a reactionary called Sipyagin, in St Petersburg in April 1902. After this many young supporters of the Social-Revolutionaries (S.-R.s) were convinced that systematic assassinations of major officials of the regime would inspire a peasant revolution and bring the destruction of the regime. The 'Basic Theses' of the S.-R.s envisaged systematic political terror as a crucial part of a concerted programme of worker and peasant actions, demonstrations, and risings.

> Their terrorism is intended not only to help disorganise the regime, but also to serve as a means of propaganda and agitation which will display itself before the eyes of the whole people, which will undermine the prestige of governmental power, which will prove that the struggle is really possible, and which will bring alive other revolutionary forces. Finally, all the secret revolutionary party find terror a means of defence and of protecting the organisation against espionage and treason. ([127] p. 67)

This excerpt from 'The Basic Theses' succinctly states the tactical objectives of the terrorism which in the early 1900s constituted the major activity of the party, and which absorbed most of their money, energy, and personnel. It should be stressed that the final function of terrorism listed (i.e. defence against treason and espionage) was not of purely secondary significance. For though the S.-R.s did not develop any really new techniques of terrorism beyond the methods of assassination already used by the People's Will, they did now confront a much more sophisticated secret police in the shape of the

Okhrana with which it became locked in deadly combat. The leaders of the Okhrana became pioneering specialists in techniques of surveillance, infiltration, and *agents provocateurs*.

Conspiratorial organisations working against the secret police in autocracies are especially vulnerable to infiltration and corruption by their enemies. This is partly because the regime has no limits placed on these activities by independent judicial or parliamentary organs. But it is also due to the inherently dangerous nature of the revolutionaries' work. No one who appears willing to work devotedly for the cause will be readily discarded. Not only are terrorists difficult to physically replace, they know too much to be allowed to run free of the tight conspiratorial network. All terrorist revolutionaries depend ultimately on mutual trust and the loyalty of each of its members to the organisation. The S.-R.s were betrayed by informers repeatedly at all levels. But their greatest disaster was the rise of a double agent planted by the Okhrana, Azev, to the position of head of the Battle Organisation [106]. This period in S.-R. history illustrates vividly those dangers which Vera Zasulich had earlier sensed to be inherent in an exclusive dedication to terrorist conspiracy – the risk that an activity calling for criminal techniques would be taken over by the criminally-minded instead of led by idealists, and that the concentration upon murder and dissimulation would corrupt the very heart and mind of the revolutionary movement.

We must bear in mind that the ultimate aims of the populists were libertarian and democratic. Their early programme had promised that terror would end when political liberty had been achieved ([127] p. 67). Their statements repeatedly demanded an end to autocracy and its arbitrary powers and punishments, and the granting of freedoms of speech, of the press, and of assembly. Social-Revolutionaries would have agreed with the earlier *Narodnaya Volya* that terrorism was indeed only justifiable as the final resort of revolutionaries fighting a despotism. (In November 1881 the journal *Narodnaya Volya* had denounced the assassin of President Garfield on the grounds that America was a democracy with free elections and liberties of expression. In such a society political assassination was 'the manifestation of a despotic tendency'.)[16] The S.-R. journal *Revolutionary Russia*, no. 7, inveighed against those who argued for exclusively terrorist tactics. Terrorism was to be properly linked and co-ordinated with the broader revolutionary strategy, and 'Terrorist acts must be carefully organised. They must be supported by the party which directs their action and will assume moral responsibility for them' ([127] p. 155).

The Battle Organisation was extremely exclusive and, under Gershuni's leadership, it probably consisted of between a dozen and fifteen members, all of whom were dedicated professional revolutionaries in constant readiness for terrorist action. Yet outside this exclusive body there were those who were strongly critical of the Battle Organisation's increasing autonomy, who feared the eclipse of the Party's political role. And there were splinter groups who favoured a combination of peasant agitation and armed risings with more campaigns of local 'economic' or 'agrarian' terror against local landowners and businessmen. Some felt this would build up more revolutionary strength among the masses than the centralised campaign of terror against distant and easily replaceable political figures. Under Azev's direction, however, the Battle Organisation became virtually a law unto itself and planning was carried out by Azev and his terrorist committee acting as a dictatorship within the Party. The eventual unmasking of Azev, as the result of persistent investigation by an alert Party member, was a body blow to the morale of the Party. Spiridovich is possibly understating the case when he describes the central committee as 'perplexed and indecisive' at the news. They did, as a matter of course, pass a death sentence on Azev (they were unable to carry it out as he had escaped), but they seemed unable to recover their nerve and energy, and by 1911–12 their terrorist organisation had become a shadow of its former self. So much depended on the existence of a few dedicated individuals with the will and revolutionary commitment to attract and recruit new members and to train them for terrorism. Unfortunately for them they could not produce a new Gershuni to pull them together: they

[16] For a translation of the full text of the declaration, see T. G. Masaryk, *The Spirit of Russia*, trans. E. and C. Paul (London: Allen & Unwin, 1919) p. 545, no. 26.

lacked a magnetic and forceful personality to organise the young terrorists into a group who believed themselves to be superior and dedicated beings, 'a priesthood . . . beyond reach and question of the laity of the party' ([113] p. 213).

It is not our object to trace the detailed histories of these revolutionary terrorist movements. It is essential, however, to identify the major strands of revolutionary movement, their ideologies and their tactical and organisational innovations. Among the most important influences are anarchism and nihilism. These are often associated with Russian struggles largely because, as one authority observes, 'the writings of Bakunin with their emphasis upon violence as a method of achieving social change were the inspiration if not the actual source of this doctrine' ([55] p. 577). Yet although Mikhail Bakunin (1814–76) was a Russian, his ideas were far more influential in southern Europe, especially in Spain and Italy, than in Russia itself, though as we shall see there were some bizarre manifestations of pure nihilism in the 1860s in Russia, and small anarchist groups began to burgeon in western and southern Russia in the early 1900s. Nevertheless, the main thrust of Russian terrorist activity against autocracy was organised by populist revolutionaries who were only marginally influenced by Bakunin and his self-appointed apostle, Nechayev. The basic statement of the principles espoused by Bakunin and Nechayev (probably authored by the latter) is *The Revolutionary Catechism* (1869).

The *Catechism* describes the essentials of the revolutionary terrorist organisation: it was to be made up of secret cells composed of individuals ready to sacrifice themselves for the Revolution. It advocated infiltration of all institutions of the state the better to undermine them, and the stirring up of discontent among the peasantry in order to provoke mass insurrection. Individual terror was advocated and to determine those who should be executed:

The comrades should draw up lists of the condemned, in order of their relative evilness, keeping always in mind the success of the revolutionary cause. . . . The first we destroy must be those men who most endanger the revolutionary

67

organization – those whose sudden and violent deaths would most frighten the government and weaken its power by depriving it of energetic, intelligent officials. (Quoted in [47] p. 8)

The predominant theme of *The Catechism* is *destruction* of the existing order. Unlike the populist socialists, the anarchists and nihilists did not attempt to sketch in detail the better society which would, supposedly, replace the existing order. Sergei Nechayev, who had begun to make contact with student revolutionaries in St Petersburg in the 1860s, travelled to contact Bakunin in Geneva. Nechayev persuaded him that he had formed an impressive network of revolutionary cells throughout Russia and he extracted from Bakunin a membership certificate for the 'General Committee of the European Revolutionary Alliance' (an entirely mythical body) signed by Bakunin. With this invaluable accreditation, Nechayev returned to Russia and proceeded to build up The People's Vengeance, a secret society run on Bakuninist lines. Sergei Nechayev appears in the guise of Verkhovensky in Dostoyevsky's *The Possessed*. At one point Liputin (one of the conspirators) asks Verkhovensky: 'One thing; only tell me the truth. Is there only one group of five in the world, or is it true that there are several hundred of them?' Peter prevaricates at first and then answers: 'You're a fool, Liputin. What difference could it make to you now whether there's only one or a thousand?' ([33] p. 604).

As we have noted, it was in western Europe that Bakunin's ideas and tactics of violent insurrection were most influential. Though he had broken with Marx and Engels and the First International he was by no means without influence and he left groups of militant anarchist sympathisers wherever he journeyed. Hence anarchism, as distinct from pure nihilism, took firm root in parts of France, Spain, Austria, Italy and even the United States (where it was spread mainly by European émigrés) between the 1870s and the 1890s. But anarchism proper and its ideas of the value of 'propaganda of the deed', developed by Bakunin and later by Kropotkin, did not have its full effect in Russia until the period from 1905 to 1914. In Europe and the United States the major debate among anarchists concerned the justifiability of violent means, especially terrorism. But we must remember that in most cases they were debating tactics that would be appropriate in anarchist struggles against *liberal democratic* regimes, and we will be considering their work more closely later. Interestingly enough, their contribution to the fight against autocracy in Russia and eastern Europe was quite insignificant [8]. The largest Russian anarchist group, the *Chernoznamentsy* (the Black Banner movement), appears to have been seeking a utopia of the kind sketched by Kropotkin, a society of communes in which individuals would be rewarded according to their needs. They tended to draw heavily upon the support of students coming from the ethnic minority groups. Among their tactical innovations were: indiscriminate 'general' terror; thefts of weapons from police stations, arsenals, etc.; 'expropriations' of funds from banks and offices; and 'economic' terrorism against businessmen and industrialists and their premises. A rather wilder, more anti-intellectual group were the *Beznachalie* ('Without Authority'), who favoured what they called 'motiveless' terror and regarded any murder as a 'progressive action' ([8] p. 50). As for Kropotkin, he was ambivalent about violence and terror. On the one hand he claimed that random murders could do nothing to change the existing social order. Yet on the other he was prepared to justify 'defensive terror' against repression, 'propaganda of the deed' to awaken the masses, and acts of violence stemming from passionate feeling for the oppressed ([74] pp. 5–9). Like the S.-R.s the anarchist groups suffered from the intensification of police repression under Stolypin's emergency measures. Those who were caught could expect no mercy from the courts-martial which handed out summary executions.

We have already noted that Plekhanov's Social Democrats did not favour terrorist tactics. The Mensheviks who later split with the Bolsheviks took the same original S.D. line. The Bolsheviks' attitude was rather more complex: they did not believe in individual assassination as a practical revolutionary strategy, but they did believe in the ultimate necessity for mass terror in a revolutionary situation and Lenin's term for this was 'armed struggle'. Prior to the revolution the Bolsheviks used 'expropriations' to build up their funds, and were much criticised for this by the Mensheviks, but they did not indulge in individual terror. Indeed, after the 1905 reforms introduced by the tsar, the way was opened for all parties to organise for electoral purposes in order to contest seats in the Duma, and Lenin and his Party were to make full use of tactics of legality in building up their organisation and their support. Lenin believed that the most important lesson that Marx had taught revolutionaries, in his analysis of the failure of the Paris Commune of 1871, was the vital necessity of smashing the bureaucratic–military machine of the state ([97] pp. 106–7). The Bolsheviks carefully prepared infiltration of the armed forces as part of their tactics for the seizure of state power and acts of random terror had really no part in Lenin's hard-headed calculations, as he made clear in 'Partisan Warfare' [80]. As a means of overthrowing autocracy individual terrorism was, in Lenin's view, worse than useless. It lost valuable lives of courageous revolutionaries and provoked a thorough-going repressive response by the government which only made difficulties for the mass revolutionary organisation.

Having identified the major ideological influences, organisations and tactics involved in the Russian struggle against autocracy, we can now address ourselves to some problems of general analysis. First, how was the theory and practice of terrorism transmitted to succeeding generations of revolutionaries? As already noted, the universities were in a true sense the nurseries of terrorism in nineteenth-century Russia, and students also played an important role in terrorist organisations in eastern Europe. In Russia tsarist policy towards the university system oscillated between encouragement and reaction. By 1860 the gradual removal of restrictions on university entry had brought many poverty-stricken students to St Petersburg and the other centres, and desperate overcrowding of the universities ensued. The student societies seethed with discontent about their immediate conditions and alarmed the government by claiming rights of political expression and organisation not only for the students but for the Russian people. The government responded by deciding to cut back on the number of scholarships and by closing down some universities. St Petersburg students rebelled against the new policy, and so the government closed down the St Petersburg and Moscow universities for two years. This is an early illustration of the syndrome of student turbulence/government repression which has characterised all modern autocracies, as instanced by the many recent clashes in Spain, Greece, and Chile. The sociologist Lewis Feuer [41] has made an interesting attempt to link this syndrome of student revolt with a general theory of generational conflict, and he has offered an analysis of the motivations underlying student participation in terrorism in nineteenth-century Russia.

Feuer points out that many of the Russian students who rallied to the 'going-to-the-people' movement in the 1870s were children of the nobility, thereby showing that 'their ethical consciousness was utterly independent of class interests and class position' ([41] p. 4). When the student activist was rejected by the peasantry 'he would often find in terrorism a sort of synthesis for thereby he could assail a social institution . . . and hurl against it all the aggressive passions which menaced himself' ([41] p. 6). According to this theory student terrorism is thus a product of the students' desperate feeling of isolation combined with their propensity for romantic idealism, self-sacrifice, nihilism and their self-perception as a heroic elite. Feuer sees student terrorism as expressive of inner 'psycho-ethical' needs and generational hatreds rather than as instrumental to any rational and practicable political goals. This hypothesis seems to have the merit of explaining the otherwise apparently irrational aspects of Russian terrorism, the readiness of young people to undertake acts which risked almost certain capture followed by death or life imprisonment (after the execution of Sofia Perovskaya the tsarist regime decided not to carry out the death sentence against women revolutionaries) – which otherwise could only be explicable in terms of a death-wish. It is also true that, to a large extent, the mid-nineteenth-century student bodies were practically the only group able to shake free for a few years from the rigid Russian class divisions to become a kind of natural breeding ground for revolutionary brotherhood.

Yet we must be careful to qualify this theory of student

activism to take account of changes in the social composition of the Russian university population in the period from 1860 to 1914. By the end of the nineteenth century the university diploma had become the vital ticket to upward social mobility and the bulk of students comprised the *raznochintsy* and the children of the middle classes. Now the newer lower-class student elements tended to flock to the expanding technical institutes and to vocationally-oriented university studies. The data available to us concerning the political activism of students in Russia early in this century seem to lend support to more recent sociological findings on student politics in many countries [83]. It is clear that the overwhelming majority of upwardly mobile students tended to be politically inactive, more involved in problems of study and student welfare, and reluctant to associate themselves with any confrontation with university authorities. The student activists who were the mainstay of the Social-Revolutionaries and other revolutionary groups formed a tiny minority of the overall student population. Over a third of these were drawn from the children of the professional middle classes and higher officials, and there was a preponderance of activists following literary and philosophical studies ([41] pp. 115 ff.). It was this small but significant minority who provided the true nursery for the Social-Revolutionary Party's terrorism which reached its crescendo of violence in 1906–7.

One is therefore inclined to be somewhat sceptical of Feuer's sweeping Freudian generalisations about the 'revolt and guilt of the primal sons' in Russian politics, his implication that terrorism was basically unconsciously motivated and therefore predetermined. Why was it Russia and eastern Europe in particular which manifested this concentration on terrorism in the nineteenth century? And by what special processes were the tiny terrorist brotherhoods recruited and sustained? As we have already observed, the Social-Revolutionary leaders did not see themselves as the passive playthings of pathological politics. They believed in the efficacy of systematic terrorism as a *political* weapon to be abandoned only when their populist and libertarian objectives had been attained. What are these additional factors which cannot be supplied by Feuer's theory of generational revolt? Firstly, there was the special character of

72

Russian cultural history, the isolation and elitism of the Russian radical intelligentsia and its long tradition of involvement in conspiratorial societies and its commitment to revolutionary change. Each new movement for 'land and liberty' arises from the embers of the old. Nor must we, secondly, underestimate the influence of charismatic revolutionary personalities who were almost literally worshipped by the young people whose company they sought and whom they recruited and trained for terrorism. The will-power, determination and leadership of people like Zhelyabov, Vera Figner, and Gershuni were literally the only forces that kept populist terrorism alive in the darkest periods of crack-down by the autocracy. Gershuni was perhaps the last of these truly charismatic figures among the S.-R.s. Spiridovich pays tribute to his qualities of sincerity, intelligence and an iron will, and notes his hypnotic power of converting the young to his cause ([127] p. 149). Finally, there was the real personal hatred felt by the revolutionaries for so many of the officials and ministers of the autocracy, especially chiefs of police and prison governors well known for their brutality. Invariably the terrorists' statements issued after an assassination listed, in general terms, the victim's 'crimes' against the people and the revolution. Many terrorist acts were motivated by the desire to avenge a comrade.

How politically effective is terrorism as a weapon against autocracy? By itself it is patently unable to achieve a revolution. It should have been obvious to the Russian populists that even after the assassination of the Tsar himself in 1881 all that happened was his replacement by a monarch who was even more autocratic than his predecessor. The autocracy closed its ranks, the Black Cabinet and the Third Division were given more men and money, repression of all radical opposition was intensified, and the moderate advisers like Count Loris-Melikov were elbowed out in favour of ultra-reactionaries in the Pobedonostsev mould. Thus pure terrorism against autocracy is potentially self-defeating. Lenin and Trotsky were greater political realists in recognising that terrorism's only useful role was as an auxiliary weapon in the final showdown with the regime, the mass insurrection and the revolutionaries' consolidation of power. Moreover, the corrupting and distorting effects

73

of revolutionary terrorism upon its practitioners are all the more serious when all energies and finances are channelled into assassination to the neglect of mass agitation and organisation. Vera Figner, the veteran terrorist, ruefully admitted that terror 'arouses ferocity, develops brutal instincts, awakens evil impulses and prompts acts of disloyalty. Humanity and magnanimity are incompatible with it.'[17] It would be an exaggeration to say that terrorism was alone responsible for the failure of the radical intelligentsia to acquire genuine liberal-democratic convictions and sentiments. (After all in eastern Europe many of those who had made their early political careers in terrorism for national liberation became true bastions of democratic constitutionalism when independence was attained in the inter-war years.) What did happen was that movements which became almost exclusively terrorist, such as the Russian S.-R.s between 1905 and 1908, thereby disabled themselves from playing an effective or constructive political role in democratic reform.

C. LIBERATION FROM FOREIGN RULE

It is impossible to exaggerate the importance of struggles for national freedom as settings for revolutionary terrorism. If one were able to suddenly magic away all outstanding problems of ethnic subjection, grievance and irredentist feeling, most of the problems of terrorism by movements and factions would vanish with them. One leading specialist in 'counter-insurgency' operations has admitted, with unconscious irony,

> Without question, in the most successful revolutionary wars of the last 25 years, the strongest appeal has been to nationalism and patriotism based either on resistance to a conqueror or the gaining of independence from a colonial power. Once the strength of the [revolutionary] party has been built up on such a basic cause, then subsidiary causes of a more specific political or economic nature . . . can be developed to appeal to particular sections within the community. ([134] p. 6)

[17] Cited by Feuer [41] p. 108.

74

Yet we must be careful of assuming that every instance of perceived ethnic hostility or sense of injustice or oppression will necessarily be translated into revolutionary warfare: 'The leap from conditions sufficient for revolution to revolutionary warfare itself is a perilous one' ([36] p. 232). Nor can we take for granted the autocratic character of all political systems subjected to ethnic revolt. Liberal democracies such as Canada, the United States, and the United Kingdom, for example, have all recently suffered to some degree from both ethnic group violence and terrorism.

Struggles for national liberation are by no means invariably accompanied by terrorism even as an auxiliary weapon. In India, although terrorism was endemic in certain areas throughout British rule, the major resource of the independence movement which eventually carried the day, the Congress Party, was a strategy of non-violence, civil disobedience and mass demonstration. Terrorism played a negligible role in Mao's guerrilla revolutionary struggles in China, in what could be described as a semi-colonialised regime, from 1937 to 1949, and only a relatively small proportion of the Chinese population became victims of repression during the period of Mao's consolidation of power. In the transition of British colonial Africa to independence in the late 1950s and 1960s most of the nationalist movements attained their objectives by political pressure and negotiation. It is probably true that this process was facilitated by the British experience of one large-scale terroristic guerrilla struggle which frightened the colonial authorities badly, by the Mau Mau in Kenya. But it was, of course, expedient for Britain, in her straitened post-war circumstances, to lower the imperial flag as swiftly as possible. Hence the map of British Africa was mainly revolutionised by diplomacy instead of war and terror, except in the south where white settler regimes entrenched their racist supremacies. Most of Latin America won independence from Iberian colonialism by insurrection and conventional armed struggle. In short, resort to revolutionary terrorism has been the exception rather than the rule in the recent history of anti-colonial struggle. It was used against Britain in Ireland, Palestine, Kenya, Malaya, Cyprus, and Aden, on a major scale. And it is noteworthy that in each of these cases the situation was more complex than a contest for a colonial 'hand-over', because the British found themselves involved in a triangular conflict involving inter-ethnic or sectarian struggles in each of these areas. Terror was used quite extensively against the French in Indo-China, the Dutch in Indonesia and versus the Americans in the Philippines, and very extensively against the French in Algeria. It was widely adopted as a partisan or guerrilla auxiliary weapon against German and Japanese occupation forces in the Second World War, and has been similarly employed against Portuguese colonial regimes in Angola and Mozambique. In nearly all these instances the occupying regime's forces have deployed repressive terrorism against the indigenous popula-tions and in many cases it is brutal terrorism against guerrillas which *inaugurates* the cycle of terror and counter-terror.

The nationalist and national-revolutionary ideologies that have inspired or justified guerrilla struggle can easily be deployed to rationalise the use of terror tactics. Among guerrilla partisans there is rarely any intense moral debate about this. As Gross remarks, in relation to the Poles' use of terror against Russian rule, the legitimacy of using any means against a hated foreign invader seems to be almost unquestioningly accepted and resort to terror is not usually accompanied by tormented philosophical debates ([52] p. 442). At the same time a lack of ideological sophistication may be a sign that the basis of the insurrection is really one of common hatred of the foreign 'enemy', and there may be little or no common agreement as to political objectives, even no agreed definition of national identity and appropriate frontiers, for example, as was the case in the Internal Macedonian Revolutionary Organisation (I.M.R.O.) from 1893 to 1934. Moreover, as a number of authorities on nationalism in Asia, the Middle East and Africa have emphasised, it is a serious mistake to apply European models and theories of nationalism in Third World contexts [71, 101, 125, 142]. There are passages which vividly illustrate the cultural divides involved in the autobiography of the Indian terrorist, Damodar Hari Chapekar (collected in [71] pp. 397–461). Chapekar felt most resentful against the English, not so much for clearly-articulated political reasons, but because of

76

the humiliation and subjection he felt he and his religion suffered at the hands of the English colonial government. It was an article of faith with him and his brother that their highest calling as young men was to become warriors. They applied to the government to be allowed to join the Army, and when rejected:

I said to my brother that we might make one more application [to government] stating: 'Since you decline to appoint to suitable posts men like ourselves, who are fond of the art of war, how should we gratify our desire? Should we rebel?' Considering that the making of such an application would be tantamount to open hostility, we decided that since the English were our implacable enemies and the cause of our subjection, we should commit as many hostile acts against them as we could. *This was the first and the most potent cause of the enmity between the English and ourselves* [my italics]. ([71] p. 421)

What drove Chapekar and his brother and friends to terrorism was exasperation at what they regarded as sacreligious offences against the Hindu religion and the sullying of their martial honour. Among those whom they considered to be proper persons 'on whom we might inflict punishment' were an educated Hindu who had embraced Christianity, and an English official who offended against their code by organising a municipal house-to-house inspection by soldiers in a campaign against bubonic plague, and whom they assassinated for his pains. The sophistications of the nationalism of Congress intellectuals are entirely beyond their understanding or sympathy. Indeed they regard with especial suspicion an Indian-nationalist movement claiming English intellectual supporters!

It was inexplicable to us how those very Englishmen who in this country send us to lifelong transportation for the mildest unfavourable comments [upon the acts of government] could permit Messrs. Hume, Bradlaugh and others of their own race to remain alive in England even though they have incited us [to act] in opposition [to government] . . . I, therefore, began to consider how, in the face of the above facts, this was possible. And I came to the conclusion that all this was a sham and nothing more. I was convinced that those people were acting under the instigation of our wily administrators and had come forward to deceive the Hindus and to give a harmless turn to their activities with a view never to allow their thoughts to turn towards deeds of cruelty. ([71] p. 406)

Frequently, therefore, terrorism against aliens is the product of traditional xenophobia, religious zeal and atavism. In Asia, the Middle East and parts of Africa there are many examples of sectarian terrorist assassinations by no means confined to attacks on foreigners. These traditionalist and religiously moti-vated terrorists are, however, capable of learning unexpected lessons from the fate of the explicitly political movements and their leaders. Sainrakhio, the Hur, who, with his colleagues, fought a lengthy terrorist campaign in the Sind region against the British in the name of his religious leader Pir Saheb, records that:

When Pir Saheb had discussions with Congressmen in jail, he learned how, whenever their leader, Gandhi, was imprisoned by the government for inciting them to break the law, they would create violent disturbances all over the country, and persisted until the government grew tired, and was glad to release Gandhi and so be free of the trouble. So when our Lord happily returned to us, and had proceeded out of ear-shot of the police . . . he addressed the Hurs . . . and put them to shame, reminding them how when he was arrested they had sat at home like women; whereas the followers of Gandhi, on his arrest, raised such a fire throughout Hindu-stan, Gujarat and elsewhere that the government repented; and yet Gandhi was a person of infinitely smaller consequence than himself. ([77] p. 40)

In such unforeseen ways are the practices of terrorism diffused!
Nevertheless, despite these connections between tradition-alism, religion and individual acts of terror, the most important and widespread form of political terrorism employed in struggles for liberation from foreign rule has been that which is

systematically deployed by revolutionary leaders as an extension of the strategy and tactics of guerrilla warfare. 'Guerrillas' is a term of Spanish origin, used to refer to small bands of irregular or partisan troops which have been used to fight campaigns of attrition, harassment, and hit-and-run ever since war began. Every example of national-liberation terrorism used in our discussion exemplifies it as an extension of guerrilla tactics. This does not mean, of course, that guerrillas universally employ terrorism, or even agree with it in principle. Unless it is extremely carefully supervised and selective (i.e. directed at unpopular senior officials) it can rebound on the guerrillas by alienating the popular support which they depend upon, thus drying up the sea in which the guerrilla fish must swim. In any event, there is always the risk that terrorism will provoke heavy retaliation by security forces which could wipe out guerrilla cells and capture supplies which have been gathered by months of patient work by the revolutionaries. As Guevara argues:

> It is necessary to distinguish clearly between sabotage, a revolutionary and highly effective form of warfare, and terrorism, a measure that is generally ineffective and indiscriminate in its effects, since it often makes victims of innocent people and destroys a large number of lives that would be valuable to the revolution. . . . Many consider that its use, by provoking police oppression, hinders all more or less legal or semi-clandestine contact with the masses and makes impossible unification for actions that will be necessary at a critical moment. ([53] p. 26)

Debray, however, accords it a role of limited value; 'of course city terrorism cannot assume any decisive role, and it entails certain dangers of a political order. But if it is subordinate to the fundamental struggle (of the countryside), it has from the military point of view a strategic value; it immobilizes thousands of enemy soldiers in unrewarding tasks of protection' ([30] p. 74). Now this comment of Debray's is interesting from another point of view; because of its unquestioned assumption that terrorism is *urban*, in contrast to the guerrilla struggle which is *rural*. It is foolish to assume that systematic murder, bombings and selective or indiscriminate terror are mainly confined to cities. Many organisations from the I.M.R.O. and the Dashnaks to the I.R.A., F.L.N., and Vietcong have shown that political murders and even general terror can be waged in the countryside with less fear of intervention by the government forces, and with ruthless effectiveness. Village headmen have been 'executed' on a large scale by the Vietcong, and there have been many cases of collective 'punishment' by the burning and shooting up of villages in Indo-China, the Middle East and Africa. Nor should we be confused by the pejorative journalistic use of the term 'terrorist' to apply to all insurgents. There *is* an important distinction between guerrilla warfare, whether rural or urban-based, and terrorism. Guerrillas may fight with small numbers and often inadequate weaponry, but they can and often do fight according to conventions of war, taking and exchanging prisoners and respecting the rights of non-combatants. Terrorists place no limits on means employed and frequently resort to widespread assassination, the waging of 'general terror' upon the indigenous civilian population, and even the killing of innocent foreigners who may never have visited the country of the revolutionaries. We shall attempt to keep these distinctions clearly in mind in examining and comparing some liberationist movements that have employed terrorism. First we consider traditional ethnic and republican-nationalist struggles in Europe, illustrated by the Macedonians and the Irish. Following this we turn our attention to some more recent anti-colonial nationalisms, and finally to the communist-led revolutionary struggle to reunify North and South Vietnam by 'liberating' the South from 'American Imperialism'.

The Internal Macedonian Revolutionary Organisation (I.M.R.O.) formed its central committee in 1894 to concert action to liberate Macedonia from the Ottoman Empire. The basis for the Organisation had been created at Ressen in 1893 on the initiative of Péré Tocheff and Damian Grueff. The slavic name for the rebels was *hajduk*, but the Turks called them the *komitadji* because the local organisations were run by committees. The *hajduk* were originally the outlaws of legendary bravery and romance who raided the Turkish settlements from

their mountain retreats. The I.M.R.O. and its young intellectual leaders (mainly drawn from school-teachers in Turkish
Macedonia) joined up with the outlaws and learnt from their
tactics while the *hajduk* in turn developed the rudiments of a
political consciousness and a programme. The only friendly
state to which they could turn for aid against the Turks was
Bulgaria, whose independence had been confirmed by the
Treaty of Berlin (1878): Rumania was too far away to help.
Many Macedonians had settled in Bulgaria, where they played
a disproportionately influential role in the government, army
and the professions, and many Macedonians studied in central
and eastern European universities where they inevitably encountered the ideas of the nihilists, the Bakuninites and
Narodnaya Volya. Not unnaturally they began to conspire to use
these methods against their Turkish oppressors.

The I.M.R.O. had grave handicaps in addition to its geographical isolation. Macedonia was a multi-ethnic region
which included Serbs, Greeks, Jews, and Kutzo-Vlachs, as well
as Bulgars. Were they to form a nation of their own? Should
they be merged into Bulgaria? Should some kind of Balkan
federation be set up? From the beginning there were two major
factions, one favouring the incorporation of Macedonia into
Bulgaria, and the other proposing a Balkan Federation with an
autonomous Bulgaria. All they could certainly agree about was
their hatred of Turkish rule which, by all accounts, was
extremely oppressive. The *beys* ruled with great arbitrariness,
and the Christian Macedonians were heavily taxed and were
discriminated against in every aspect of their lives. Frequently
they were subjected to the raids of Turkish soldiers who often
behaved lawlessly and cruelly towards the local population.

From their inception the *komitadji* showed themselves to be
partisan-guerrilla fighters of skill, courage, and toughness, but
they could only harass their opponents by hit-and-run attacks,
briefly taking over towns and villages, seizing weapons and
funds and then retreating to their bases. They could sting and
injure but they could not totally destroy their enemies. The
organisational structure they established between 1895 and the
Balkan Wars anticipated, in many respects, the partisan resistance organisations of the Second World War. They were a

secret society organised on highly disciplined lines with local cells of about ten members each, and a secret army with a political directorate in the form of the Central Committee. Though the forms of democracy were supposed to be observed, and its programme called for a liberal-democratic Macedonia, in practice the organisation was run like a command structure. In addition it had a tax collection system and its own courts and secret police which it used ruthlessly against those who breached discipline in the I.M.R.O. From the early days assassination was used against individual Turkish officers and officials, and the retaliation of the Turks was savage, often resulting in the destruction of whole villages in the troubled regions; thousands of Macedonians fled to Bulgaria.

Terror was also carried into the cities of Salonika and Skopje. A group of young students organised a terrorist group at Tirov Veles and they were influenced by the ideas of a dedicated terrorist called Merdzhanov who had been won over to terrorism by Russian populist and anarchist ideologues. After an abortive attempt to blow up branches of the Ottoman Bank in Salonika and Constantinople simultaneously, these young men eventually waged concentrated bombing campaigns in Salonika and Skopje. These had the effect of provoking brutal retaliation by the Turks, but they did not win liberation for Turkish Macedonia or the sympathy of the major powers. Gradually the influence of the pro-Bulgarian faction within the I.M.R.O. grew and, largely through their pressure, Bulgaria joined the Central Powers against the Serbs in the First World War. They managed to keep Bulgarian policy rigidly opposed to the establishment of the new post-war frontiers of Yugoslavia, but the price they paid for having been on the losing side was that much of Macedonia was placed under Serbian control. The I.M.R.O. constantly harassed the Yugoslav frontier, aided by funds and support both from Bulgaria and the Italian Fascists, in a desperate bid to annex all Macedonia. Neither guerrilla raids nor terror bombings designed to pressure major capitalist powers achieved their objective.

Failing in its major political objectives, the I.M.R.O. began to turn inwards, concentrating its efforts on establishing a virtual 'government' within a state in Bulgaria, engaging in a factional war of assassinations, and intimidating the Bulgarian government. No politician could safely walk the streets of Sofia without an armed bodyguard; every businessman felt the squeeze of the I.M.R.O.'s insatiable demand for 'dues'; even the restaurateurs and grocers were terrorised into free provisioning of the hungry 'pensioners' of the I.M.R.O. The factions of the movement led by Alexandroff, Protogueroff, and later Vantche, engaged in a murderous gang war in the streets, often catching innocent passers-by in their fire. In an early anticipation of the contemporary international terrorism they extended their murder hunts and gang war to Vienna and Milan. Prime Minister Stambuliiski, leader of the Peasant Party, tried to act against the *komitadji* to protect the Yugoslavian border. In retaliation the Minister of War, a district prefect, and later Stambuliiski himself, were murdered. Alexandroff, the leader of the main I.M.R.O. faction, was murdered in 1923, and by the late 1920s the Protogueroff faction and the Mihailovists were battling for control of the terrorist satrapy. The I.M.R.O. had come full circle and had forsaken revolution for the ancient sultanism of the Turks, whose empire they had set out to challenge [84, 117, 138].

One of the most important factors that caused the Macedonian liberation struggle was the inspiratory example of neighbouring Bulgaria's independence. If the Bulgars could enjoy the fruits of autonomy, freedom for their religion and culture, and careers open to the talents, why should not the Macedonians enjoy the same status? Young Macedonian intellectuals experienced a revolution of rising expectations, but lacked the resources or capabilities to fulfil them. In nineteenth-century Ireland violence against the British-controlled government had started in a haphazard and spontaneous fashion much earlier. It broke out spasmodically in the Fenian terrorism of the 1850s and 1860s, backed considerably by aid from the American Fenians. But despite the legal and land-holding disabilities of the Irish peasant, and the endemic poverty and distress of the mass of the Catholic population, the government of Ireland in the nineteenth century was neither so brutal nor so repressive as that of the Turks in the Balkans. It was still possible for Irish nationalists to express their objectives and to organise openly for the purposes of peaceful reform within the framework of the constitution. Therefore the main thrust of Irish political nationalism was expressed in the mass campaigns of O'Connell and Parnell and the Irish nationalist M.P.s at Westminster. With Gladstone and almost half the Liberal Party apparently on their side and later attempting to push Home Rule through Parliament, this strategy seemed to be the right one. The calls of the Fenian Irish Republican Brotherhood for violent revolt appealed only to a tiny minority of Irishmen who took the secret society's oath: they were stronger in American support than they were in Ireland itself, although it is true that a small brigade under John MacBride went to fight with the Boers against the British in 1902. The overwhelming majority in Ireland was, however, still in favour of achieving Home Rule by constitutional reform through Westminster. This was favoured by the Irish Party under Redmond. Unfortunately for Redmond and his colleagues the Home Rule Bill eventually approved by Parliament in 1914 was shelved owing to the exigencies of the First World War and the bellicose intransigence of Carson and his Ulster volunteers, who threatened to resist Home Rule by force to 'protect' the interests of the Presbyterian protestant majority in Ulster.

How was it that the Irish came to abandon the constitutionalist strategy and resort to the violence of the Fenians? Why did Ireland become involved in a full-scale war against the British forces between 1918 and 1921? How did the Irish Republican Army come to replace the Irish Nationalist Party as the major force in the South? In part it was due to an increasing sense of disillusion about Home Rule, and a real doubt that the Tories would ever allow it to be implemented without a struggle. Anti-English feeling was also intensified by the attempt to introduce military conscription throughout Ireland. Also, well before 1914, the revolutionary-minded nationalists of Sinn Fein (Gaelic for 'Ourselves Alone') were busily infiltrating organisations like the Gaelic League (an organisation for cultural nationalism) and the other cultural and political institutions in the South and forging links with the nascent Labour Party under James Connolly in Dublin. Above all, there was an increasing sense of threat felt in response to the development of the Ulster para-military force and its huge imports of weapons and ammunition. Surely, many argued, the South must arm itself if only for defence; 'The Irish Republican Brotherhood, meeting in secret, had decided that to fight the new danger, the only method was to bring about the creation of a Nationalist Volunteer force to counter-balance the Ulster Volunteers' ([123] p. 326). They believed the I.R.B. label would frighten off many recruits, so an umbrella organisation, the Irish Volunteers, was formed at the instigation of Eoin MacNeill and Roger Casement. It was explicitly justified in the manifesto, launched at the opening recruiting campaign in November 1913, as a self-defence organisation. In MacNeill's words:

> The object proposed for the Irish Volunteers is to secure and maintain the rights and liberties common to all the peoples of Ireland. Their duties will be defensive and protective, and they will not contemplate either aggression or domination. Their ranks are open to all able-bodied Irishmen without distinction of creed, politics or social grade. . . .[18]

The alignment of para-military forces in Ulster and the South was accompanied by frenzied attempts to build up arms supplies on both sides, and in 1913 leaders from the North and South were looking to Germany as a potential source of arms. In the South and especially the area in the south-west the spirit of Fenianism was reviving rapidly: the cultural patriots, the romantic intellectuals of Irish nationalism, had now found the means of fitting out their dream with uniformed young men and rifles. After the Curragh Mutiny, when it became clear that the government could not rely on the army to act against armed resistance to Home Rule in Ulster, support for Redmond in the South was gradually ebbing away.

Undoubtedly, the major cause of the shift towards revolutionary violence was the Easter Rising in Dublin in 1916. This insurrection was led by men such as Padraic Pearse, James Connolly, Joseph Plunkett, and Thomas MacDonagh, whose nationalist beliefs were fanatical, almost religious. Only the

[18] From a speech by MacNeill cited in [123].

most ardent idealists could have gone into such a reckless and dangerous enterprise with a handful of men confronting the whole of the British garrison and the police forces. They must have known that their own capture and death were almost certain. The Dublin population greeted their revolutionary proclamation and seizure of the General Post Office with an almost derisory disbelief. There was no mass uprising behind the rebels. After six days the Rising collapsed, though not until both sides had suffered considerable casualties. Four days after the rebels' surrender the authorities issued the following statement at Dublin Castle: 'The three signatories of the notice proclaiming the Irish Republic, P. H. Pearse, T. Mac-Donagh and T. J. Clarke, have been tried by Field Court-Martial and sentenced to death. The sentence having been duly confirmed the above three-mentioned men were shot this morning.'

Further executions followed, and out of a total of 160 convicted for their part in the Rising, fifteen were executed and ten were sentenced to life imprisonment. The Irish authorities had created a new roll of Irish martyrs, and as a direct result Irish nationalist opinion became decisively alienated against British policy. In 1918 Sinn Fein was able to win resounding successes in the elections against Irish Nationalist Party competition, and by late 1919 local guerrilla forces of the Irish Republican Army were in action with increasing frequency against Royal Irish Constabulary and British Army units.

Tom Barry, in his account of his experience with the West Cork Flying Column, admits the revelatory effect of the Easter Rising events upon his own political consciousness ([9] pp. 9–11). Barry had been serving with the British Army in Mesopotamia when he first read the news of the Easter Rising and the ensuing executions. The news came to him like a bombshell, driving him to read all he could about Irish history and the events leading up to 1916. Literally, for Barry and many others, 1916 was a discovery of national identity and it provided them with a cause to fight for. In this sense the rising can be said to have succeeded both as a work of art (see [135]) and as a brilliant stroke of propaganda. After the Republican victory in the 1918 General Election, the new Dáil Eireann (Irish

Parliament) proclaimed *de facto* independence and set up its own government of Ireland. By so doing they brought themselves into a state of war with the British government. But there were still many Irishmen who did not share the heady, idealistic, atavistic romanticism of Pearse and the cultural nationalists. Some still hoped for a negotiated constitutional settlement; a small Protestant minority supported the militant Unionists in the North; and a rather larger minority could not relish the prospect of a grim war which seemed to be both a struggle for national independence and a civil war rolled into one. Seumas Shields, the pedlar, in O'Casey's play *The Shadow of a Gunman*, was speaking for many when he was made to say:

It's the civilians that suffer; when there's an ambush they don't know where to run. Shot in the back to save the British Empire, an' shot in the breast to save the soul of Ireland. I'm a Nationalist meself, right enough . . .; I believe in the freedom of Ireland, an' that England has no right to be here but I draw the line when I hear the gunmen blowin' about dyin' for the people, when it's the people that are dyin' for the gunmen! . . . ([108] p. 132)

The main tactics employed by the I.R.A. were those of guerrilla harassment, raids on police stations, arsenals, military posts and barracks and ambushes mounted by the famous Flying Columns against numerically superior and better armed British Forces. Michael Collins, one of their leading strategists, developed the use of selective terror against the security system. He believed that, as soldiers were easily replaceable and as general terror of the civil population would alienate public support, it was most important to reserve assassination for intelligence officers and high-placed police officials, whose knowledge was vital to the authorities and whose experience made it impossible to adequately replace them. This was the rationale behind the murder of thirteen out of sixteen special intelligence officers sent specially to Dublin to track down Collins himself. In addition to this use of individual terror, Collins concentrated special care on a counter-espionage system which infiltrated practically every government office and police department in the country, and which effectively crippled the effectiveness of the security forces' activities. The I.R.A. also used terror against those suspected of informing within its own ranks, but it did not adopt a policy of indiscriminate civilian terror. Collins himself appears to have been a political realist whose clear political objective was to secure an independent Ireland. He showed political flexibility and realism by accepting the terms of the Anglo-Irish Treaty in 1921. (His acceptance was crucial in carrying the Treaty with the Irish negotiators.) He clearly believed dominion status and, in practice, independent government for all Ireland except Ulster, were worth settling for in the circumstances of 1921. The I.R.A. was, after all, not a huge force as some British military men had mistakenly assumed. At its largest it probably comprised about 15 000 men. It was short of weapons and, despite firm support from the American Irish, Collins realised it would be extremely hard-pressed to survive the more determined and large-scale onslaught threatened by Lloyd George if the Treaty was rejected.[19]

But the guerrilla and terrorist war in Ireland was not easy to stop. For many in the professional 'Flying Columns' it had become a way of life. Like the Macedonians of the I.M.R.O. they had become inured to the life of the outlaw–gunman. They could not see why the maximalist demand for an entirely independent and completely unified Irish Republic could not be realised; many were anxious to continue the struggle. Many of those who fought for the I.R.A. had known no other life since their demobilisation from the First World War: many had been unemployed or came from the small peasant-farmer class. There were few who felt impelled to return to the routine of ordinary civilian existence. The Republican hard-core of the I.R.A. fought a bitter and protracted struggle against an Irish Free State Army (largely equipped with British weapons). Even when they eventually conceded defeat they continued as a clandestine force concentrating much of their effort on aiding their 'brothers' in Ulster (the Republican element in the Catholic minority) to organise against the Ulster Unionist regime. (The post-1967 development of the I.R.A. struggle in

[19] For the important role played by Collins see [133].

Ulster is considered on pp. 115–20.) The small, close-knit para-military and clandestine nature of the I.R.A. organisation since the 1930s has facilitated its use of the weapons of terrorism, both in Ulster and the Republic and, for brief periods, in England. Like the I.M.R.O., it has suffered from proscription by the government of its native country. In the 1920s and more recently it has been dealt with by Special Powers Acts of considerable severity. It has also manifested, in common with the I.M.R.O. and many other long-lived terrorist movements, very deep and sanguinary internal schisms [23]. Although it could be argued that in the I.R.A. the Irish created a destructive force which they were unable to tame, it is nevertheless an important fact that its tactics in the struggle for independence, its blend of guerrilla and terrorist techniques, proved extraordinarily effective in reducing the will of the British to stay in Ireland. And this lesson was certainly not lost on nationalist leaders elsewhere; especially it attracted those movements which lacked the military strength or external aid to mount a full-scale war. Guerrilla terrorism increasingly, though not exclusively, became the favoured weapon of the weak.

The majority of moderate Zionists in Palestine under the British Mandate did not believe in the need for an I.R.A.-type of guerrilla–terrorist organisation for the Jews. They supported the self-defence organisation, Haganah, to protect Jewish areas and the kibbutzim, but they did not believe in mounting an aggressive war against the Arabs or the British. Leaders like Weizmann and Ben-Gurion had set their hearts on gaining a Jewish state through diplomatic negotiation. Jabotinsky, founder of 'Revisionist' Zionism, Menahem Begin, Raziel and their supporters did not accept this non-violent strategy and advocated carrying war into Arab territory in reprisal for Arab attacks during the worsening ethnic conflict in the late 1930s. In 1936 Jabotinsky and Begin founded the Irgun Zvai Leumi (National Military Organisation), a secret guerrilla–terrorist organisation roughly a thousand strong, modelled on a miniature I.R.A. Like the I.R.A. it was initially ultra-nationalist in ideology and had more in common with the far Right than with the Left. Begin taught a strict asceticism, pride in Jewish religion and history, and operated a rigid military code of discipline. The Irgun had a para-military structure; sections at local level, divisions for regions, and a central command headquarters. Begin's immediate objective was the creation of an independent Jewish state with its original Biblical boundaries. The terrorism used by the Irgun, however, was more indiscriminate than that of the I.R.A. or the Russian or Balkan terrorists previously discussed. In 1938–9 they began planting bombs in Arab buses, market-places and urban areas, and always issued communiqués after each incident claiming that their action was an act of revenge for Arab violence. In reply to Jews who charged them with murder they quoted the text 'a life, for a life, an eye for an eye, a tooth for a tooth . . .'. Begin had learnt from a wide range of terrorist techniques and published the essence of his guerrilla–terrorist doctrines in *The Revolt* [10].

Most of the Irgun leaders and the moderates of the Jewish Agency believed that anti-British operations designed to force Britain's acceptance of the creation of a Jewish state should cease immediately on the outbreak of the Second World War. The fanatical Abraham Stern and his small group of followers (probably never more than 200 in total) still insisted on regarding the British colonial authorities as the major enemy, so they broke with the Irgun and formed the Stern Gang. Despite rejection by the majority of the Jewish population, and the loss of their leader Stern (killed in a shooting incident in Tel Aviv), the Gang continued to wage terror against the British. Sternists perfected the clandestine techniques of the terrorist secret society, and were organised into cells of three members only, having vertical lines of communication to the central committee. Their own tight security procedures were partly copied from those of criminal gangs. The Irgun was organised as an underground guerrilla army, its members only being armed for raids and operations. Sternists were always armed and were under orders to kill as many British as possible in resisting arrest. The Sternists' major effort was put into individual terrorist assassinations of British officials and security men. After several unsuccessful attempts against the life of the Palestine High Commissioner, they succeeded in murdering Lord Moyne, British Minister of State for the Near East, in November 1944.

Unlike the Stern Gang, the Irgun campaigned mainly by means of 'confiscations', raids on British government and military installations, spectacular ambushes, and commando-style attacks such as the famous raid on Acre gaol in May 1947. But the Irgun's selection of symbolic targets and its penchant for explosions carried the price of higher civilian casualties. It was all too easy for the Irgun to infiltrate important buildings in the cities and plant explosives: but they could not ensure that large numbers of innocent people would be warned or evacuated in time. Thus, for example, when the Irgun blew up the British Headquarters in Jerusalem at the King David Hotel, over 200 people were killed or wounded. Terrorism played a very large part indeed in impelling the British Labour Government to withdraw rapidly and to hand the problem over to the United Nations Organisation. If there had been no British withdrawal it is possible that some form of partition, or a Jewish–Arab State, would have resulted. Hence the terrorists could claim to have played a decisive role in creating the State of Israel. But it should be said that this has been at the price of war and instability in the area ever since: the Arab states and the Israelis have yet to learn to live peacefully side by side. Palestinians are still without a homeland and in their camps bitterness and hatred have nourished the twins of desperation and terrorism now meted out against Israel. For terrorism, like war, is the enemy of the politics of compromise, bargaining, trust and relative peace.

Quite clearly the record of the Irgun and the Sternists provided a fearfully tempting model for the Palestinian guerrillas who followed them. Like the Jews of the period 1937–47, they now faced, when fighting alone, overwhelming superiority of force. Like the Irgun they had relatively small forces and limited weapons. Terrorism provided, therefore, the most economical means of wreaking maximum psychological shock to Israel and its supporters, and the simplest means of gaining world-wide publicity for their cause, and of inspiring their own people to continue and intensify the struggle. Terrorism is, under these circumstances, an appealing weapon for the militarily weak and the desperate. Yet we must not underestimate the resources that were available to the Jewish terrorists. Most of the Irgun were professionally qualified and many had advanced technical expertise in engineering, weaponry and explosives. This underground army, so vividly portrayed in Arthur Koestler's *Thieves in the Night* [73], certainly had skills available to it comparable to the best European partisan organisations of the Second World War: it was well within their capacities to build lengthy underground tunnels, dislocate rail systems, mine roads, and engage in infiltration and espionage. In addition, both Irgun and the Sternists got limited but vital financial aid from sympathisers in the Diaspora (see Sacher [120]).

One could hardly imagine a greater contrast with this mainly urban-based and sophisticated terrorism than the terrorism waged by the Mau Mau secret society in Kenya in the early 1950s. This society was not founded or sustained by the black Kenyan intellectuals and students: it was essentially a tribal secret society which used terror as a protest against the European settlers who held highland farmlands which they claimed rightfully belonged to the Kikuyu. Not all the Kikuyu were involved, and there was only a small degree of overlap with the more highly politicised Kenya African Union party (K.A.U.). The veneer of nationalist feeling in Mau Mau's utterances was of the thinnest kind. Much more fundamental was its primitivism and atavism, the vaguely articulated yearning for a return to pre-colonial Africa and the welling up of hatred and barbaric violence against settlers and all Europeans. This was not a modern-style voluntarist political association of the ideologically converted: the secret society obtained many of its members by coercion and terror against fellow Africans. The initiation ritual and oath taking are well described by Josiah Kariuki in '*Mau Mau*' *Detainee* [69]. At his first oath ceremony he was the only one in his group of initiates who was not 'hit about a little'. The oath administrator held the lungs of a goat in one hand and another piece of the goat's meat in the other:

> We bowed toward the ground as he circled our heads seven times with the meat, counting aloud in Kikuyu. He then gave each of us in turn the lungs and told us to bite them. Next he ordered us to repeat slowly after him the following sentence:

I speak the truth and vow before God
And before this movement,
The movement of Unity,
The Unity which is put to the test
The Unity that is mocked with the name of 'Mau Mau',
That I shall go forward to fight for the land,
The lands of Kirinyaga that we cultivated,
The lands which were taken by the Europeans
And if I fail to do this
May this oath kill me
May this seven kill me
May this meat kill me. . . . ([69] p. 26)

The oath taking was sealed by a ritual of anointing and mingling with blood. Kariuki felt he had been given a 'splendid and terrible force'. Certainly it was terrible in its effects upon the Kikuyu. In response to a number of atrocity killings of settlers and their families, the government launched an intensive counter-terrorist operation in the troubled rural areas, resulting in an estimated 10 000 African deaths and the imprisonment of approximately 90 000 [91]. Despite its defeat, Mau Mau was in part a break with the previous patterns of tribal revolt against colonial rule. The Oath of Unity (termed 'Mau Mau' by the authorities) was designed to be administered not only to Kikuyu but also to other tribes who would make common cause with them against the European. Here was evidence of an, as yet ill-defined, wider Kenyan African nationalism. The other novel factor is that the clearly articulated major grievance of the Mau Mau, their land-hunger, reflected a genuine and deep-felt alienation among the Kikuyu against the Kenyan colonial economic structure. It was the Kikuyu who had, through proximity to the towns and relatively greater exposure to mission education, more than any other tribe developed a violent protest against the inequalities of their society. Though terrorism was not the weapon which ultimately gained them independence, it is reasonable to suggest that the British security forces' expensive and lengthy counter-terrorist campaign in Kenya helped to ram home to Conservative ministers in Britain that they had better bow before the 'wind of change'.

In the long run, Mau Mau terror was not without results; and this was despite their lack of political direction, their primitive weapons and resources, and their lack of any outside aid.

The terrorism of Grivas's EOKA organisation, which began its struggle for Enosis (Union with Greece) in 1954, had much more in common with Irish and Palestinian terrorism. In the first place they were, in large part, 'successful' in that the British colonial regime was forced to withdraw. Although Enosis was not realised, Archbishop Makarios and the bulk of the Greek Cypriot population were satisfied with the granting of an independent Republic of Cyprus negotiated in Zürich and London in 1959. Grivas had long experience of partisan–guerrilla tactics in Greece and he proved an elusive and resourceful guerrilla–terrorist leader. As in the case of the Irgun, EOKA did not really have a permanent partisan force of a scale that could defeat British forces decisively in open battle. They therefore adopted tactics of guerrilla ambush and commando-style raids from their mountain bases in the interior and combined these with terrorist operations primarily aimed at officials, policemen, British soldiers, and their families and against any Cypriots, Turkish or Greek, believed to be assisting the British against EOKA. They combined Stern-Gang-type assassinations in broad daylight with Irgun-style methods of blowing up British installations, mining roads, and destroying communications.

The similarity between the Irgun and the EOKA terrorisms even extends to their political consequences. In neither case did terrorism alone achieve their ultimate stated goals. In Cyprus EOKA had to settle for less than Enosis, and for a continued (semi-permanent?) U.N. presence to police Greek–Turkish communal relations. And the tactics of the Irgun in Palestine did not achieve a state of Israel with the original Biblical frontiers. It was the 1967 war which brought that expansionist goal of Begin's somewhat nearer to fulfilment. Yet now Israel is under intense diplomatic pressure to withdraw from the major part of these occupied territories. By late 1973 it was clear that it was neither Jewish nor Arab terror that would be decisive in shaping the power balance in the Middle East. Superpower needs for detente or accommodation, and the western powers' dependence on oil supplies from the Arab states, are the really weighty factors in the equation. Both EOKA and Stern consisted of a small hard-core of fanatics organised in tiny cells. (It is estimated that even at the height of its campaign in Cyprus EOKA terrorists numbered only a hundred or so, though it is clear that these depended extensively on sympathisers in both villages and towns.) In both Palestine and Cyprus terrorist tactics were used almost exclusively, and both groups of terrorists consciously learned from earlier examples of these techniques and tactics against the British. Crozier quotes from an address by the Cypriot Bishop of Kyrenia who said (in August 1954): 'Kenya will get its freedom because Mau Mau kills people. The English soldiers are leaving Egypt because the Arabs are every day killing them' ([27] p. 137). Leaders of the Greek Church in Cyprus had apparently no qualms about openly inciting their flock to terrorism.

One lengthy guerrilla–terrorist struggle of considerable importance and interest occurred in Malaya between 1948 and 1955.[20] The communist-led Malay terrorist campaign led by Chin Peng, like the revolutionary terrorism of Vietnam and the Philippines, grew out of the original anti-Japanese resistance organisation. After staging a brief and terrible terrorist rule for a few weeks before British rule was restored, in 1946, they retreated into the jungle and regrouped for a major terrorist assault which began in 1948, after a wave of communist-inspired strikes. The terrorist forces, according to authoritative estimates, numbered at most 8000 men. Against them, at the height of the counter-terrorist campaign, were ranged 80 000 troops and security forces with air support. Most of the terrorists were drawn from the Chinese, an ethnic minority deeply distrusted by the Malays. They did not have a secure basis of support among the rural population, mine-workers, or estate labour, because much of the Chinese population was either rootless or urban-based. Only the 423 000 or so Chinese land-squatters who had nothing to lose and everything to gain by siding with the terrorists were likely allies. Chin Peng could therefore never manage to create a popular guerrilla army as he had no 'sea' of friendly peasants in which his small terrorist

[20] For full accounts see Denis Warner [147], Brian Crozier [27], and Richard Clutterbuck [19].

bands could 'swim'. They relied upon murder raids upon estates and mine-workers and their local European and Malay and loyal Chinese officials as well as individual attacks and ambushes against the security forces. The British began to intensify security control and improve their intelligence and surveillance measures and to regroup the more vulnerable rural squatter population into armed villages which could be easily defended and insulated against Peng's terrorist cells.

The terrorists, simply because they were a small minority alienated from the bulk of the Malay population, could not concentrate sufficient military strength to enable them to dislodge government authority. Neither were they able, therefore, to terrorise enough of the people into the submission which would have given them a permanent and secure base area, despite their brutal policy of murder and abduction of the civilian population. (By late 1951 the terrorists had killed 1275 security personnel, and nearly twice as many civilians.) Indiscriminate civilian and economic terror began to rebound badly against the Malayan Communist Party which suddenly realised that terrorism was losing them desperately needed popular support. In 1951 the Politbureau of the Malayan C.P. instructed that 'to win the masses the Party must . . . stop burning villages, . . . attacking reservoirs, power stations and other public services. Rubber trees, tin mines and factories must not be destroyed because of the resentment of the workers who lose their employment' (quoted in [56] p. 38).

One of the greatest authorities on revolutionary war in southeast Asia has stressed three main conditions which both underline the *differences* between the Vietnam and Malayan insurgencies and help to explain the defeat of the latter. First, and most important, the Malayan terrorists lacked a common border with a communist power which could have given access to more weapons and supplies. Second, the terrorists always remained too narrowly based on the Chinese ethnic minority, and, third, the security forces were able to maintain a ratio of about ten to one against the insurgents (instead of the four to one more generally operative in Vietnam).[21]

[21] See Fall [37] pp. 338 ff. for an excellent comparative discussion of these campaigns.

In Algeria between 1954 and 1962 the French government and the Algerian nationalists (F.L.N.) became embroiled in a particularly bloody conflict involving countless terrorist atrocities not only by the F.L.N., but also by white-settler groups such as the O.A.S., and the colonial government and army, in a diabolical cycle of political terror. F.L.N. activists only numbered a small minority of the Arab population, led mainly by urban intellectuals, but they did secure the tacit support, if not the active co-operation, of the bulk of the Arab population in the cities, and a large following in the rural areas. The F.L.N. employed terror to secure several immediate aims. Most important was the fact that it used indiscriminate terror (e.g. bombs in crowded market places, shops, buses, stations, etc.) in order to provoke and deepen ethnic schism between European and Arab. As Aron observes, 'In the case of indiscriminate terrorism, the reaction of those of French stock is to regard all Moslems as suspect, if not to take revenge on any of them who happen to be caught. If terrorism is not selective, the repressive reprisal is not likely to be selective either. . . . The inevitable errors of repression heighten this disintegration. When too many innocents are punished, abstention ceases to seem a protection. Recruitment of insurgents goes up as risks of passivity and insurgency begin to equalise' ([6] p. 170). The terrorists capitalise on this polarisation, suspect all who are not actively collaborating with them as 'traitors', and do their best to enmesh the individual into the F.L.N. structure by making him or her an accomplice of terror and safely *hors de la loi* in the eyes of the regime. As Fanon asserts: 'The group requires that each individual perform an irrevocable action. In Algeria, for example, where almost all the men who called on the people to join in the national struggle were condemned to death or searched for by the French police, confidence was proportional to the hopelessness of each case. You could be sure of a new recruit when he could no longer go back into the colonial system' ([38] p. 67).

For the F.L.N., terrorism provided a means of carrying the struggle for an independent Algeria into the heart of the long-established settler communities. It enabled them to shock the French metropolitan government out of their apparent intransigent insistence on treating Algeria as if it were an integral part of France. Like the Irish before them, they carried their struggle into the metropolitan territory. With the aid of guerrilla units supplied and aided from the Arab sanctuaries of Tunisia and Morocco, they conducted raids and ambushes against French units and installations, blew up public buildings and tied down the large French forces who sought them. By resorting to terrorist assassinations and bombs they sowed fear and disruption in the cities and destroyed all confidence in the Europeans or the colonial authorities. Some of their murders were particularly hideous, involving throat-slitting and severing the nose, a symbol of dignity to the Algerian ([18] p. 59). An aim of the individual terror was to destroy all elements in the population, especially Muslim officials, who were sympathetic to the French or who collaborated with them as moderate leaders among the Arab community. The F.L.N.'s immediate military objectives were to prepare for a general uprising in Algiers and to make it militarily too expensive for the French army and authorities to stay.[22] Terrorism continued unabated through all the stages of the French–Algerian struggle: it was especially useful as an auxiliary weapon when the French forces had practically defeated the F.L.N. as a guerrilla force in the field. But ultimately neither guerrilla war nor terrorism, singly or in combination, could suffice to bring about French withdrawal.

What did Algerian F.L.N. terrorism achieve? In addition to the destruction of community, and the deepening of ethnic division noted above, it led to an intensification of violent conflict within the Muslim community and to terrorist combat between European settlers and Muslims. In addition to intimidating and killing the moderates, the F.L.N. also engaged in a bloody feud with Messali Hadj's Algerian National Movement (M.N.A.). F.L.N. terror is also considered by many analysts to have been both a response to French colonial repressive terror (e.g. the 1945 Sétif Massacre when over 15 000 Muslims were killed) and, in turn, a *cause* of the further upward spiral of terrorism and counter-terrorism. One analyst has stressed that

[22] See Yves Courrière's general history, *La Guerre d'Algérie* [25] vols 1–4.

the O.A.S. was, in its turn, a mirror-effect of F.L.N. violence and one which 'crowded the whole repertoire of the F.L.N. into the last violent months of French rule: murder, bombings, communal slaughter, terrorism in metropolitan France, the attempt to launch an uprising in Algiers, and guerrilla operations in the mountains' ([105] p. 55). Moss and Gaucher [47] consider that this O.A.S. terrorism was ultimately self-defeating in that it only brought a more rapid agreement between the F.L.N. and the French government, and a rush exodus of European settlers.

A second major effect was to provoke massive French governmental repression. The French army had already developed, on the basis of its Indo-Chinese and Tunisian experience, a doctrine of *la guerre révolutionnaire*. In brief, this asserted that revolutionary wars were part of a long-term communist strategy to wreck western civilisation, using indirect action rather than normal conventional war. It was important that the *series* of struggles must be won, even if individual battles had to be conceded. According to this doctrine all major western military effort should go into containing the revolutionary war, and not into nuclear arms or conventional defence.[23] Acting on the basis of this doctrine the French army began, 1954–5, to wage its own *guerre révolutionnaire* against the F.L.N. in the firm belief that this was a crusade to save the West from communism. For them Revolutionary War strategy meant a combination of guerrilla and psychological warfare methods (as they expressed it in their manuals RW = G & P). This war had to be waged with an ideological fanaticism and ruthlessness which would more than match that of the insurgents. The French government's Special Powers Act of March 1956 gave the enabling measures for a ruthless repression by the army. Special Administrative Sections (S.A.S.) were established to control 'pacification' zones into which between $1\frac{1}{2}$ and 2 million people were 'regrouped'. Ground forces in the area were increased from 50 000 to 400 000 and additional local defence forces of 100 000 men were raised. In the rural areas the army, aided by special 'gangs' of commandos operating in F.L.N. style, slowly des-

[23] For a full discussion of the French military ideas on revolutionary war, see Paret [112] and *Revue militaire d'information* [116].

troyed the F.L.N. guerrilla structure and compelled their forces to retreat to bases in Tunisia. From late 1956 the army began to purge Algiers of the F.L.N. using some of the following measures:

adoption of elaborate methods to distinguish the FLN from the rest of the population. (This involved employing large numbers of informers and infiltrators; and such techniques as the use of hooded informers to identify FLN as they emerged from the Casbah); murder raids (*râtissages*), launched against villages and quarters suspected of hiding rebels, both as a punishment and a warning to others; regular and widespread use of torture in interrogation at military detention centres and police stations; 'resettlement' (i.e. deportation) of whole populations of villages or quarters to insulate them from the FLN.

By 1960 the French army had virtually defeated the F.L.N. militarily and forced them back into a desperate campaign of urban terrorism. But although the F.L.N.'s guerrilla 'army' was beaten, the French were unable to seal their victory with any political success because they were trapped by the rigidity of their own revolutionary war doctrine. They had not fully appreciated that no revolutionary war in the proper sense of the term could be won *unless it offered something politically appealing and durable to the population*. The army had virtually nothing to offer except more coercion or public relations gestures such as community services designed to improve civil–military relations. Unlike the British in Kenya and Malaya, the French army did not offer any acceptable political set-up to the populace, and hence they could not win over or permanently secure the allegiance of the F.L.N.'s constituency of support. The F.L.N. were able to regain the initiative largely by intensive and skilful anti-French propaganda among the Muslims, and by instilling into them a fear of terrorist punishment for any acts of collaboration. The extra-legal and indiscriminate nature of the repressive measures used by the French and noted above also had the effect of cementing support for the F.L.N. and rendered the Muslim population more receptive to F.L.N.

ideology. Furthermore, it increasingly alienated world opinion against the French government's policy. The foreign pressure against the French government's military operations in Algeria, especially American pressure, contributed towards the ultimate reversal of French policy [25].

The most interesting and widely influential of the revolutionary theorists produced by the Algerian Revolution was Frantz Fanon (1925–61), a psychiatrist born in Martinique who became a revolutionary while working in an Algerian hospital. Fifty years earlier Rosa Luxemburg and Lenin showed prescience in anticipating the importance of the independence struggles of colonial peoples. Fanon, who knew what it was like to be on the receiving end of colonialism, spelt out an impassioned and damning indictment of exploitive tropical colonial regimes with their rigid racial 'compartments' and their accompanying repressive violence. Arendt is quite correct in differentiating between the role accorded to violence in Marx's theory of revolution and its place in the ideas of Fanon and others on the new Left ([5] p. 97). For Marx violence had no special intrinsic value: it might, indeed very probably would, become the necessary means or 'midwife' of revolution, but it was conceived as being an entirely temporary measure to deal with the exigencies of the revolution and the dictatorship of the proletariat. In the long term the *abolition* of political violence was to be the essential precondition for the liberation of mankind. At certain times Marx even appeared to be ready to concede that emancipation of the proletariat might be achieved by means of peaceful reform, for example in the United States or Britain. This could no longer be a serious possibility, in strictly Marxist terms, once Britain's bourgeois class had strengthened their hold on the state and society by a massive enlargement of the bureaucratic–military machine. Fanon believed, however, that the bloodiest violence should be used against colonial regimes. This was the only practicable method of smashing the ruthless and vicious dominance of European racialism. But more than this was involved: for Fanon the act of furious violence against the colonial settlers and their policemen is collectively and individually cathartic.

Individually, argued Fanon, the native re-creates himself

through violence: he regains his sense of manhood, his dignity and his identity, and purges the humiliation and injustice meted out to him and his forebears by the colonial oppressor. No longer is the native compelled to channel his anger and latent violence into magico-religious rituals and dances. Revolutionary violence enables the natives to use their superior numbers and will-power to decisively liquidate the colonial regime. Collectively this is the only possible way, in Fanon's belief, for the exploited peoples of the Third World to shake off the distorting myths and opiates of liberal individualism, to overcome the deliberate atomisation of the colonial native populations and to create a new sense of brotherhood through struggle ([38] pp. 36 ff.). It is quite clear then from many passages in *Les Damnés de la Terre* that Fanon envisaged other beneficial consequences flowing from this collective catharsis of violence; a new mass political consciousness and sense of national identity would be born, old tribal and sectarian differences would be eroded, the forces of taboo, magic and superstition would be displaced, and women would be emancipated from their traditional subjugation to participate in the work of the revolution.

In her essay 'On Violence' [5] Arendt considerably underestimates both the originality and the political importance of Fanon's writings. To be fair, most other European and American critics have accorded his work only superficial attention or have tended to distort his ideas by trying to force Fanon into the Marxist–Leninist classification. Nor should he be regarded as a romantic iconoclast purveying a Third World peasant utopia after the manner of a recent essay [17]. Firstly, there is a tendency to overlook the ambitious scope and wide appeal of Fanon's anti-colonialist ideology. He is determined to speak for the have-nots of the world, for the real Third World, from a secure and intimate understanding of the wretchedness of their situation. The struggle envisaged is not only to be waged 'in every place where colonialism means to stay on': Fanon believes it must be carried over to the offensive by confronting the ex-colonial powers *en bloc* and demanding economic justice for the wrongs done against them in the past:

We are not blinded by the moral reparation of national independence; nor are we fed by it. The wealth of the imperial countries is our wealth too. . . . Europe has stuffed herself inordinately with the gold and raw materials of the colonial countries; Latin America, China and Africa. . . . Europe is literally the creation of the Third World. The wealth which smothers her is that which was stolen from the under-developed peoples. . . . Nor will we acquiesce in the help for under-developed countries being a programme of 'sisters of charity'. This help should be the ratification of a double realization by the colonized peoples that *it is their due*, and the realization by the capitalist powers that in fact *they must pay*. ([38] p. 81)

Nor does Fanon content himself with merely stating his aggressive anti-Europeanism. He sketches various possible retaliatory measures including 'collective autarky' and withdrawal of all co-operation and supplies to the capitalist world. However uncomfortable it may be for the western powers to admit, this is the disturbing voice which finds increasing echo among all Third World countries. It would be wise to bear in mind that it is a fairly short step from angry hatred and desire for reprisals and terror in the context of a single anti-colonial struggle to a collective recourse to violence by groups of Third World countries against the developed powers.

There are two sources of considerable tension and ambiguity in Fanon's work. One derives from the collision and conflict of western and traditional values reflected in Fanon himself. On the one hand he hopes and plans for an emancipated, egalitarian and genuinely humane socialist civilisation which will have all the resources of modern medicine, science and technology so urgently needed to improve the health and living conditions of the masses in the developing countries. On the other he is antipathetic to the native urban intelligentsia, suspecting them of blind egoism, and looks to an idealised grass-roots community of peasant-guerrillas to provide the basis for his revolutionary socialist democracy. There is also a conflict between the ideological totalism implicit in his readiness to justify extreme violence and his scientific training which warned him of the

103

potentially traumatising effects of such violence on both its perpetrators and its victims. Thus he accepts that: 'The violence of the colonial regime and the counter-violence of the native balance each other and respond to each other in an extraordinary reciprocal homogeneity. This reign of violence will be the more terrible in proportion to the size of the implantation from the mother country. The development of violence among the colonized people will be proportionate to the violence exercised by the threatened colonial regime' ([38] p. 69). Yet all the while that he is helping the F.L.N. and individual terrorists to prepare themselves for their tasks he is also collecting case-histories in his psychiatric work which prove to him that 'the events giving rise to the disorder are chiefly the bloodthirsty and pitiless atmosphere, the generalization of inhuman practices and the firm impression that people have of being caught up in a veritable Apocalypse' ([38] p. 202). If it is no longer possible to pretend that violence is a purely creative and 'cleansing' force then the onus is placed upon the ideologues of terror to show that they have brought about a tangibly better life to their society and that this improvement could not have been attained in any other way.

Since attaining independence in 1962 the Algerians have spent considerable energy and money in training and aiding guerrilla movements elsewhere, especially in Africa. For example, they have provided instructors for Mozambique guerrillas, and other anti-Portuguese movements. Yet the experience of struggles in Angola, Mozambique and Portuguese Guinea does illustrate the extreme difficulty of following the examples of Algeria and Tunisia in the different conditions of southern Africa. In the Portuguese colonies it was very difficult for the guerrillas to gain a foothold in any of the main towns: neighbouring African countries were helpful in the cases of both Angola and Mozambique, yet states such as Zaire and Tanzania were not militarily strong enough to constitute a really serious threat to the Portuguese. And states such as Zambia and Malawi were hamstrung by their economic ties with South Africa, or by dependence upon the port facilities of Beira. Most damaging of all the guerrillas were often bitterly divided and weakened by inter- and intra-movement quarrels such as those between the Revolutionary Government of Angola in Exile (G.R.A.E.) and the communist Popular Movement for the Liberation of Angola (P.M.L.A.).[24] Although the murderous repressive terror of the colonial regime in Mozambique was answered by some terrorist operations by FRELIMO (Mozambique Liberation Front), the revolutionaries were still (in 1973) waging a rural guerrilla war of attrition. Although the Portuguese enjoyed a limited success with their protected villages (*aldeamentos*) programme, the guerrillas were (in 1973) preoccupying the efforts of approximately 150 000 Portuguese security forces in Mozambique.

Terrorism has been used extensively by the Vietcong in Vietnam in the name of a 'national liberation' struggle of a far more dubious nature. Following the division of Vietnam under the 1954 Geneva agreements, the North Vietnamese and the Vietcong (V.C.) National Liberation Front within South Vietnam have been fighting the South Vietnamese government (G.S.V.N.) on the grounds that it is a puppet regime of American imperialism. The V.C. claim that the G.S.V.N. has been holding down the people of the South against their wills and preventing the reunification of the country. Now despite all their rhetoric about the 'solidarity front of the entire Vietnamese people' it is quite clear that there are many elements in the South (and not just the politicians or the Catholics) who certainly do not want to be taken over by a communist government in league with the Hanoi regime. Revolutionary terrorism in Vietnam, therefore, has been especially indiscriminate, intensive, and persistent because it has been used as an auxiliary weapon in a bitter civil war, a conflict greatly exacerbated by direct American intervention and the indirect support of the North by the communist powers. It is of course true that this whole conflict has been characterised by indiscriminate acts of war terror far outstripping V.C. guerrilla terrorism in scale and destructiveness. Yet, in the context of a discussion of revolutionary terror, V.C. terrorism has certain noteworthy features. The Viet Cong have not confined terror to the initial phase of the guerrilla build-up in the South in the late fifties and early

[24] See Felgas [40] for the background to internal conflict in the movements of Angola, Mozambique and Guinea.

sixties. They have combined rural and urban, selective and indiscriminate terrorist tactics simultaneously for a wide range of objectives, and yet they have never depended upon terrorism as sufficient to win a decisive victory. In the words of one analyst they have made it into 'a highly-developed, highly-refined political weapon designed to fester unseen from within, soften resistance to the enemy that *can* be seen, and set the stage for complete collapse of the target against which it is directed' ([92] p. 2). The V.C. refer not to terrorism but to 'armed struggle' and 'executions of traitors and collaborators' in their propaganda, but the methods are those of the European, Middle Eastern and North African movements we have already discussed: for individual terror, assassination by knife, strangulation or shooting; for indiscriminate 'general' terror, mines in roads, bombs in crowded city streets and buildings.

The specific targets of V.C. rural terror have been generally village or hamlet chiefs, local leaders, and their families, because by means of these murders they remove the only protection of the government available in the rural areas. With the removal of the link with the authorities the V.C. help to insulate the local populace from government control and rapidly substitute their own parallel revolutionary administrative, quasi-judicial and tax-gathering structures (see [37]). Gradually, by taking over whole chains of villages, the V.C. planned to surround the cities with hostile bases. Selective terror in cities has been most frequently directed against policemen and G.S.V.N. officials. The main aim of general terror in rural areas has been to make the people more malleable and responsive to the instructions of the V.C., and to collectively 'punish' any community that has collaborated with the regime. General terror in the cities has the object of disorienting the population, weakening their morale and their will to resist. According to Mallin [93] the terror count was five civilians killed per day by 1960, and by 1968 and 1969, according to U.S. State Department figures, assassinations alone were running at over 6000 per year.

The V.C. used a cell structure to organise its city terrorism, the so-called Dac Cong units which deployed a network of two- or three-man cells, none of whose members were known

106

to other cells. In an effort to counter the specifically terrorist actions of the V.C., the G.S.V.N. used sudden security sweeps, house to house searches in whole sections of the cities, road blocks and car searches. They also launched the *Chieu Hoi* or Open Arms programme to try to assist V.C. members to defect. This involved grants of money, food, and clothing to bona fide defectors with bonuses for any weapons brought in, a scheme closely modelled on the amnesty offers of the Malayan campaign. Like the terrorists of the Malayan Communist Party in the 1950s, the V.C.s also began to realise that indiscriminate terrorism could become counter-productive by alienating vital popular support. Mallin [93] publishes a captured V.C. Directive dated 24 December 1965 which admits that 'mistakes' had been made 'in our task of repressing counter-revolutionary elements' and demands that these be rectified. Too many, including many innocent people, had been arrested and killed or punished, and many had been savagely executed. According to the directive, punishment was henceforward to be used more discriminatingly, and clemency and leniency were to be shown towards those who were genuinely repentant or who could be corrected by 'thought reform'. This would suggest that, despite the flexible role accorded to terror in Vietnamese guerrilla doctrines, their leaders are well aware of its dangers and limitations as a political weapon in revolutionary civil war.

D. RESISTANCE AGAINST TOTALITARIANISM

Totalitarian political regimes are those which attempt with some success the total control and mobilisation of the population for purposes and tasks determined by the ruling Party leadership. They are thus quite distinct from the ordinary autocracy or dictatorship which simply outlaws or suppresses open opposition. Totalitarian ruling parties attempt to control the thoughts as well as the lives of their citizens, and use elaborate systems of secret police surveillance and infiltration and an army of informers to prevent the establishment of any critical or independent group even of a purely cultural or intellectual nature. Internal political opposition of any kind must therefore be necessarily a highly dangerous clandestine activity, while planning armed violence against the regime is generally suicidal. The experience of domestic resistance against both Nazi Germany and Soviet Russia shows that the totalitarian regime by definition monopolises all violence and terror within the state. Kaplan's attempt to assassinate Lenin occurred well before the Soviet dictatorship had become totalitarian. And the bomb plot of July 1944 against Hitler would have been, if it had succeeded, an act of tyrannicide rather than of terrorism. All too often the resistance against Hitler took the form of agonised and interminable political discussion of future plans and general principles within tiny circles, most of which had sympathetic contacts abroad (see [49] for a discussion of National Conservatives, Socialists, and the Kreisau Circle). Public acts of resistance, such as the scattering of anti-Hitler leaflets by the brother and sister Scholl in 1943, brought terrible reprisals from the authorities. The real tragedy of the domestic resistance to totalitarianism is that it is so alone, for the bulk of the population are readily mobilised by the regime against them. And even those who privately question their rulers are usually too frightened to give any active help to the resisting minority.

It is a different matter when a totalitarian regime attempts to maintain control over newly conquered countries. Despite the presence of collaborator elements, the bulk of the conquered population will nurse a hatred of the alien invader. They will recall the freedoms and traditions enjoyed prior to occupation and will more readily throw themselves into the active work of partisan resistance. The ferocious energy and striking power of the partisan struggles against the Nazis is documented in a number of well-known histories (see [42, 56]). These partisans frequently resorted to guerrilla terror and urban terror including assassinations of German officers, as well as general sabotage. Yet such resistance was really part of a wider struggle for national liberation throughout western and eastern Europe. In the eyes of the partisans the totalitarian nature of the Nazi political system was, in a sense, immaterial. Any alien rule was unacceptable. The history of partisan resistance in conquered lands does not therefore weaken our case that terrorism has not proved to be a viable form of struggle for domestic opposition to totalitarian rule. This is because the totalitarian leadership possesses overwhelmingly superior force and control over communications and media. Totalitarian leaders are unencumbered by any humanitarian or judicial considerations and crush dissent with relentless effectiveness. Significantly the most likely threat of internal violence against the totalitarian regime is likely to derive from an attempted *putsch* by a group within the elite who have part of the military or terror apparatus at their disposal.

E. TERRORISM AGAINST LIBERAL DEMOCRACIES

Liberal democracy is a fairly recent (nineteenth-century) development which in theory provides ample scope for political opposition and participation within the law. Compared to colonial regimes and autocracies the established western liberal democracies have been relatively free of large-scale revolutionary violence, but they have not proved to be immune against revolutionary terrorism. Liberal democracies have been particularly vulnerable when weakened by ethnic or religious conflict, by military defeat, by major economic crisis or by an erosion of popular support for democratic values. Those liberal democracies that rank among the transitional or modernising nations are, inevitably, under much greater social and economic stress. Their difficulties are exacerbated by shortages of resources, expertise and popular legitimacy, and such regimes are particularly open to terrorist attack. The intrinsic freedoms of the democratic society make the tasks of terrorist propaganda, recruitment, organisation, and the mounting of operations, a relatively easy matter. There is ease of movement in and out of the country and freedom of travel within it. Rights of free speech and a free press can be used as shields for terrorist defamation of democratic leaders and institutions and terrorist incitement to violence. If the government is provoked into introducing emergency powers, suspending habeas corpus, or invoking martial law, it confronts the paradox of suspending democracy in order to defend it. There is always the risk that by using heavy repression to crush the terrorist campaign the authorities may alienate the innocent mass of citizens caught up in the procedures of house-to-house searches and interrogations.

As noted earlier, many of the early Russian and Balkan terrorists were committed to the establishment of liberal democracies in their own countries. They believed that once that goal had been achieved terrorism would be unnecessary. Already, however, in the late nineteenth century a small minority of revolutionists was dedicated to overthrowing all forms of government, and this included liberal democracy, which they regarded as a device by which the bourgeoisie exploited, manipulated and oppressed the masses. This group were followers of Bakunin's International who believed that peaceful educational or cultural propagation of anarchism was not enough. In the last decades of the nineteenth century a small following of those anarchists who believed in acts of violence as 'Propaganda by the Deed', such as Brousse in France and Malatesta in Italy, launched a series of assassination attempts and explosions. Third Republic France, which had a liberal democratic constitution by the standards of the day, was subjected to a spectacular wave of anarchist terrorism in the 1890s. Anarchism acquired a certain *cachet* among a small minority of romantic and literary intellectuals in late nineteenth-century France. They were influenced partly by Paul Brousse (who was converted to the principle of anarchist violence in 1877), by the propagandists of the ill-starred Saint Imier International, and by the urgings of Andrea Costa who was ironically later to become an influential campaigner for reformist social democracy in Italy [129]. Also important were the anarchist journals such as *L'Étendard révolutionnaire*, *Le Droit social*, and *L'Hydre anarchiste*.

In his classic study Woodcock suggests that intellectuals, particularly the Symbolists, were attracted to anarchism partly because it appeared to stand for 'freedom of action' and 'experience for its own sake'. They also found a 'terrible but intriguing sensationalism in the lives of the [anarchist] assassins . . .' ([156] p. 306). But the anarchists who committed acts of terrorism in France at this period were by no means confined to students and middle-class professionals. Ravachol (real name Koeningstein), the most notorious of them, worked within the criminal underworld and lived in poverty for most of his life. Like Sebastien Faure and Elisée Reclus he seems to have genuinely believed that property was immoral. He believed that by robbery, forgery and other criminal acts he was helping the anarchist cause of destroying the prevailing order. With accomplices he was responsible for murdering Jacques Brunel, an elderly miser, and robbing him of 15 000 francs. Ravachol did use some of the proceeds to help families of anarchists who had been given punitive sentences for resisting arrest after organising a demonstration; and he later blew up the homes of the President and the Prosecutor of the court which had meted out the harsh sentences. He shouted 'Vive l'Anarchie!' when sentenced to death for the murder of Brunel.

Equally famous symbolic terrorist acts of this period in France were Auguste Vaillant's bomb attack on the Chamber of Deputies in December 1893, Emile Henry's bombing of the Café Terminus as an act of revenge for the execution of Vaillant, and the assassination by Caserio of President Sadi Carnot for the latter's refusal to pardon Vaillant. Vaillant's bomb did not kill, but Henry's caused one death and injured twenty people. Yet Henry expressed regret that more had not been killed and at his trial he maintained his anarchist justification: 'I wanted to show the bourgeoisie that their pleasures would no longer be complete, that their insolent triumphs would be disturbed, that their golden calf would tremble violently on its pedestal, until the final shock would cast it down in mud and blood' ([65] p. 137).

But what the terrorism in 1892–4 in France really shows is the self-defeating nature of such violence in a relatively homogeneous and stable democracy. The assassination and the explosion were not a magic formula for revolution. The general public saw such acts as sensational crimes. They achieved no more lasting political effects than the deeds of Malatesta in Italy or those of Most, Fielden and Goldman in the United States. If they had been centrally planned and co-ordinated acts (and the evidence is that they were not) they could have constituted a more serious threat. As Joll points out, the plethora of small close-knit anarchist groups made the task of police investigation extremely difficult ([65] p. 147). But the cases of French anarchist terrorism clearly exemplify the futility and the psychopathic character of acts of random individual terror in a democracy. Their immediate consequence was a severe government repression of anarchist movements and journals, *les lois scélérates*, which nearly eliminated anarchism as an effective force in France ([156] p. 314). There is no doubt that such events helped to create a widespread prejudice against anarchism and its adherents throughout Europe and the United States. The Sacco and Vanzetti trial in the United States is not an isolated example of known anarchist sympathisers being convicted for murder on the flimsiest circumstantial evidence. However, although it would be grossly unfair to equate all anarchism with terrorism, it is true that some groups have blended anarchist and revolutionary socialist ideas in a quite explicit justification of revolutionary violence. For example, the self-styled Angry Brigade, formed in 1970 in Britain as an offshoot of the First of May Revolutionary Solidarity Commitee, deliberately espoused a strategy of revolutionary violence and fostered contacts with continental anarchist and revolutionary socialist students from whom it obtained both explosives and expertise. The Angry Brigade Communiqué Number 6 declared: 'No revolution was ever won without violence. Just as the structure and the programmes of a new revolutionary society must be incorporated into every organized base at every point of the struggle, until, armed, the revolutionary working class overthrows the capitalist system.'[25]

Just as anarchists have never been able to agree about the justifiability of resorting to violence in democracies, so the revolutionary Left has been divided as to the appropriate means and moment for arming the 'revolutionary working class' against 'bourgeois' states. In particular, as we have already noted, they have been divided on the question of the role of terrorism in the revolutionary struggle. In broad terms the Bolsheviks believed that carefully directed acts of terror could serve as a valuable ancillary weapon in the actual seizure of power. Lenin and Trotsky believed it had a specially vital role, however, in the period of consolidation when they believed it was imperative to use terror on behalf of the revolutionary class in order to liquidate 'counter-revolutionary elements'. As Trotsky stated it: 'The Red Terror is a weapon utilized against

[25] Quoted in *The Times*, 7 December 1972.

a class, doomed to destruction, which does not wish to perish. If the White Terror can only retard the historical rise of the proletariat, the Red Terror hastens the destruction of the bourgeoisie' ([140] p. 64). But although belief in terror against the counter-revolution was common ground among the revolutionary left, they continued to vacillate regarding the precise role of violence at the *pre-revolutionary* stage in the bourgeois democracies. Lenin in his pamphlet *The Infantile Disease of Leftism in Communism* (Moscow, 1920) came out in favour of revolutionary opportunism, of using tactics of electoral party competititon and legality in order to hasten the onset of a revolutionary situation. Communist parties in democracies have favoured a combination of industrial militancy, electoral struggle and revolutionary propaganda and have eschewed terrorist conspiracy. Only a tiny minority of ultra-left groups have rejected these methods in favour of terrorism, against liberal democracies.

One of the most interesting and innovative of these groups in recent years has been the Tupamaros, who mounted a campaign in Montevideo, Uruguay. The name Tupamaros is derived from a rather unpropitious hero, the Indian caudillo Tupac Amaru, who was captured and executed by the Spaniards after staging an Indian agrarian rebellion in 1780. Raul Sendic, a socialist law student, started up the movement in 1962–3. Sendic spent a period as a trade union organiser among the sugar-cane workers but became disillusioned with union and party organisations. The Tupamaros soon broke formal links with the socialist party and determined on the unusual course of confronting the most securely established liberal-democratic regime in Latin America with an urban guerrilla campaign. Apparently they believed that they had to destroy the capitalist economic structure of Uruguay in order to bring about a redistribution of wealth on a revolutionary scale and thus eliminate the poverty of both city and countryside. As there was no jungle terrain suitable for rural guerrilla operations, they decided upon urban guerrilla action in the capital where half of the population of Uruguay live. In fact urban guerrilla is a more precise description than terrorist, for the movement claims that it only killed in self-defence in gun-battles with the police until early 1970 ([107] pp. 38, 47). Their favourite operations have been kidnappings of Uruguayan leaders, foreign diplomats and businessmen and 'expropriations' through bank raids. According to Núñez they have tried to avoid harming innocent victims because this would turn the people against them. Their main objectives have been to weaken the regime's support by provoking the government into harsh and unpopular repressive measures, and to reveal to the people the corruption and weakness of the regime and the desirability of a socialist revolution.

At the height of its influence in 1970, the Tupamaros probably had over 3000 members active in Montevideo, compartmentalised into 'firing groups' of four to five men, and most of these were of professional middle-class origin. The apparent respectability of its 'cover' has baffled the Uruguayan police, and made the Tupamaros cells hard to detect. Some of its raids have the black theatrical style of the Beznachalie (the Russian anarchists who often assembled in cemeteries on the pretence of mourning). Forty or so Tupamaros raided the town of Pando, twenty-one miles from Montevideo, disguised as members of a funeral cortège. In less than fifteen minutes they raided the police station and telephone exchange, and robbed the four banks of over a quarter of a million dollars. In the course of some of their raids they shot and killed police officers in street gun-battles. In 1970 they 'executed' their hostage Dan Mitrione, a U.S. AID official, in retaliation for government refusal to exchange political prisoners for him. Other murders followed as the net of police repression tightened around them. By 1972 most of their leaders had been captured, imprisoned or shot; it was especially difficult for the Tupamaros to slip away in the absence of any friendly pro-revolutionary regime on Uruguay's frontiers. Thus, despite its sensational operations and its Robin Hood publicity touch, the Tupamaros movement was unable to achieve a revolutionary takeover in Uruguay. In any case it lacked the ideological sophistication, the necessary mass support, and the armed strength to achieve a takeover. What it has helped (with roaring inflation) to bring about is a drift away from liberal democracy towards authoritarianism. It provided the nuisance value and the excuse for the ultraconservatives to intensify repressive measures against the Left in general. Nevertheless, the Tupamaros' techniques of kidnapping foreign officials and bargaining for prisoners have been widely emulated by other revolutionary groups, and the movement did deliberately promote similar tactics in neighbouring guerrilla movements through aid and advice ([105] pp. 220 ff.). Apart from their dramatic logistic operations (weapons-thefts and expropriations) their propaganda operations are especially noteworthy. They set up their own mobile transmitter to counteract their exclusion from the media and would often seize canteens or meeting halls with captive audiences to put over their revolutionary propaganda ([105] p. 223).

A far more serious threat to liberal democracies was the terrorism of the counter-revolutionary Right, the fascist leagues and para-military movements which aimed to seize state power in many European countries between the world wars. Terroristic subversion and murder was used by the ultra-Right in Weimar Germany against Rosa Luxemburg, Karl Liebknecht, and some of their comrades on the Left and also against Centrist figures such as Walter Rathenau. The Nazis later developed individual and mass terror as auxiliary weapons in combination with electoral propaganda, intimidation and infiltration, as 'normal' instruments of political power. And in Italy the murder of the socialist deputy Matteotti (1924) was one of a series of terroristic acts by the Mussolini regime in the course of its consolidation of power. Frequently the fascistic terrorist movements of the Balkans and central Europe were aided and promoted by the Nazis and Italian fascists, and based their appeal on ethnic irredentism: examples were the Croatian Ustashi organisation founded by Ante Pavelich with the aim of establishing a separate Croatian state, and the Rumanian Iron Guard, an anti-semitic and ultra-nationalist movement founded by Codreanu in 1924. The Ustashi were responsible for the massacre of a large number of Serbs and even established a concentration camp for Serbs in Slovenia (see [139]).

We have noted earlier that the political culture and tradition of Ireland have been steeped in violence. From the 'Peep O'Day Boys', the Ulster Volunteer Force, the Fenians, and the I.R.A., fresh generations of gunmen have emerged in the North and

South. As Conor Cruise O'Brien has remarked: 'Young people in both parts of Ireland have been brought up to think of democracy as part of everyday humdrum existence, but of recourse to violence as something existing on a superior plane, not merely glorious but even sacred. Resort to violence, that is, in conditions resembling those that spurred the Founders into action.'[26] In so far as I.R.A. violence has been directed against the British government since 1970 in order to force a British withdrawal from Ulster and the destruction of the Unionist regime it must be described as a campaign against a liberal democracy. But it must be admitted that, ever since the establishment of the Unionist regime in Stormont in 1922, the Northern Catholic minority has suffered from political, social and economic discrimination. Moreover, the Special Powers Acts introduced in Ulster in 1922 gave the government sweeping powers to suppress any unwelcome forms of political opposition. The outlawed I.R.A. did attempt a campaign of bombings and attacks on policemen and soldiers in the North from 1956 to 1962, but it was an ignominious failure. The political initiative among the Catholics in the North was taken by the Civil Rights Association in the late 1960s, using non-violent demonstration, petition, and political pressure. The I.R.A. was compelled to involve itself in this political work to avoid complete isolation. Apparently blind to the real grievances of the Civil Rights movement, the hard-line Unionists interpreted the movement as the front for an I.R.A. conspiracy and revolution. Self-styled 'loyalists' and the Royal Ulster Constabulary over-reacted against Civil Rights marches and demonstrations, while the Rev. Ian Paisley whipped up a campaign of anti-Catholic hatred comparable to that of Titus Oates. There is little room for doubt that the hard-line Unionists mistook the angry rioting in Londonderry's Bogside in 1969 for a Fenian rising. And the Scarman Tribunal produced abundant evidence of the panic over-reaction by the Royal Ulster Constabulary. As the civilian death-toll in the street-fighting rose, the Londonderry and Belfast Catholics began to arm themselves and to look to the I.R.A. as the only available armed Catholic defence organisation. The I.R.A. leadership in

[26] Article in the *Observer*, 12 December 1971.

116

Dublin were caught off guard by this escalation into armed conflict. They had, after all, recently swung over to a *political* strategy in the North. It was the 'Provisional' I.R.A. who moved in rapidly in 1970 to fill this vacuum. Led by hard-line 'physical force' men like Sean MacStiofáin, the Northern Republicans began to rally to the Provisional organisation because they were ready for military action, and the Provisionals became bitter rivals of the so-called 'Official' Marxist-dominated I.R.A. for the support of Northern Catholics. The Officials have felt driven to compete in offering a military response to the British security forces, but have deplored the indiscriminate nature of Provisional terrorism, and claim to attack only military targets. In fact they have been responsible for murdering a number of Ulster politicians and have frequently been involved in sectarian feud and murder against Provisionals.

It is worth keeping in mind that Belfast is almost ideal terrain for the urban terrorist. It is a city of over 400 000 people, most of whom live in small homes in narrow streets. There are few natural boundaries within the city, and because of its featureless anonymity it is relatively simple for the terrorist to evade patrols and merge into his surroundings. Much of the property is Victorian or Edwardian, and yards are divided by high walls. There are ideal fields of fire in every street, and countless hiding places for sniping and ambush. Nor is there any shortage of privately held guns, many of them officially registered on the pretext of 'rifle club' membership. Both the Provisionals and the Ulster Defence Association and the U.V.F. have obtained up-to-date arms from abroad. The Provisionals have benefited from considerable financial aid from Republican sympathisers in the United States, and from expropriations and 'donations' within Ulster. They have been able to obtain the highly accurate gas-operated American armalite rifle, made in Japan under licence for the Japanese Self-Defence Force! Some weapons, including Soviet-made rocket devices obtained from Arab states, have probably been smuggled in by sea, although the interception of the *Claudia* showed the risks involved for the gun-runners in such an operation. Certainly the border with the Republic is in constant use by the Provisionals both as a source of arms and ammunition and as an escape route for terrorists. It has proved impossible to seal the frontier effectively. Even helicopter patrolling by the army is useless in bad weather or at night – even when aided by searchlights. The U.D.A., U.V.F. and the Provisionals have been supplied with explosives smuggled in by sympathisers from the Scottish minefields, and there is some evidence that anarchist and revolutionary socialist groups have been prepared to supply explosives to both sides in the conflict, presumably in accord with Bakunin's dictum that 'the passion for destruction is a constructive passion'. In sum, all these conditions have been conducive to an extraordinarily protracted and bitter ethnic–sectarian feud between the extreme Republicans and the extreme loyalists, and a war of attrition waged by the Provisionals with the aim of compelling the British Army to withdraw.

Ideologically the Provisionals' campaign has been callow in the extreme. Their single idea is apparently to unite the thirty-two counties of Ireland into a single republic by force and terror. It is true that for a time (until late 1971) they appeared to be actually gaining militant recruits and could depend on widespread sympathy among the Catholic population. The widespread Catholic hatred and resentment of the internment measure introduced by Faulkner's government in the summer of 1971 helped to fuel support for the Provisionals. By late 1972 this sympathy had been largely eroded by the revulsion against the particularly indiscriminate and bloody campaign of bombings in Belfast and Derry which hurt the innocent civilian population (Catholic and Protestant alike), ruined livelihoods, and which seemed to prove to the bulk of the population the absolute necessity of a continuing British military presence. By continuing a stubborn policy of death and destruction the Provisionals were forfeiting all possibility of participation in, or real influence upon, the planning of a new constitutional structure for Northern Ireland to replace the now discredited Stormont system. Cathal Goulding's assessment of Mac-Stiofáin[27] could really be applied to the Provisional movement as a whole: 'The thing that I have against him is that he is a very narrow man and he is a man who won't accept or examine

[27] Given in a *Sunday Times* interview, 12 September 1971.

new ideas and in his rigidity he is sure that there is only one solution to this problem and that is by physical force. He has no time for politics of any kind – and a revolutionary who has no time for politics is in my opinion a madman.' There is no doubt that the Provisionals have deployed an impressive range of terrorist techniques including murder, dynamiting, gaol-breaking, letter-bombing and kidnapping. However, they have yet to show that they can win wide popular support in the North and South of Ireland, or that they can take *political* initiatives. Their demonstrated capability in carrying terror bombings into London and other English cities may in fact be evidence of their political bankruptcy, weakness, and despera-tion. (After all, the I.R.A.'s last bombing campaign in Britain between 1938 and 1940 also occurred when the movement had been decisively beaten in Northern Ireland.) As we have noted earlier in the cases of movements such as the I.M.R.O. and the O.A.S., terrorism can sink to the level of a corrupted and pro-fessionalised form of crime which is finally self-destroying. Nor have the U.D.A. or the other Protestant extremist organisations in the Province any better record. Several recent studies have carefully documented the large scale of their record of murder and destruction, and show how they also have actively incited to violence and promoted sectarian hatred and bigotry (see [13, 32]).

The case of terrorism in Northern Ireland further supports my argument that liberal democracy is only seriously threatened by revolutionary terrorism when there is a general withdrawal of popular support from government, or when government appears entirely unable to deal with the problems that face it. This reassuring conclusion should not lead us to neglect the tragic costs of terror in a democracy: community values are des-troyed; families are divided and bereaved; children are brought up in an atmosphere of suspicion and hatred and, in their teens, are socialised into terroristic violence. Normal business and industry becomes impossible and new investment ceases. Whole sectors of cities are so damaged by terrorism that they take on the appearance of a land subjected to air attack. Political relations between parties and groups become poisoned, so that bargaining and compromise are instantly identified as

119

'betrayal'. Both extremes take on organisational forms and attitudes of para-military movements. It becomes increasingly difficult for the ordinary citizen to escape the terror of one or other of the armed camps. 'If you are not with us you are against us' becomes the rallying cry. Terrorism can corrupt and corrode democracy by establishing a kind of tyranny over men's souls, and no democracy worth the name can afford to tolerate it.

F. INTERNATIONAL AND SUB-REVOLUTIONARY TERRORISM

Acts of terrorism which are committed for ideological or political motives but which are not part of a concerted campaign to capture control of the state may be described as sub-revolutionary. The possible motives underlying such acts may include: symbolic defiance of, or protest against, a specific act of policy; desire to avenge a death or injury inflicted by a government; summary 'punishment' of a particular locality or individual; or a belief in the intrinsic value of acts of nihilistic destruction and/or self-immolation. Alternatively, such acts may be committed by members of feuding groups who choose to take 'the law' into their own hands. Impelled by a sense of obligation to avenge and a sense of group liability, they may act terroristically. The militant suffragette followers of Mrs Pankhurst provide an example of a group which claimed to have democratic aims, but which argued that because women were denied political rights extreme violence was justified [115]. As one of their slogans declared 'Who Would be Free Themselves Must Strike the Blow'.

More generally, however, organisations resorting to sub-revolutionary terrorism have tended to be ideologically extreme, xenophobic, or racialist. Such groups usually claim to use extreme violence only in 'self-defence'. For example, in 1965 Robert Shelton, leader of United Ku-Klux-Klans, declared, 'We don't advocate violence. If someone steps on our toes we are going to knock their heads off their shoulders' (quoted in [43] p. 142). The fiery cross of the Klan has been a symbol of terror in the United States for over a hundred years. Forster

120

notes that as early as 1871 a Congressional investigation found the Klan to have been responsible for a campaign of shootings, hangings, mutilations and whippings (mainly of Negroes) in the South ([43] p. 143). Between the world wars the Klan built up a membership of four million, acquired some political influence in the North and South, and fostered links with pro-Nazi organisations with which it had much in common. In recent years they have continued to persecute and intimidate, but have selected the Civil Rights movement and 'communists' as their most frequent targets.

The Sons of Freedom sect of the Doukhobors provides an instance of a group which has practised terrorism both as part of its way of life and as a repudiation of the laws of the states with which it came into conflict. The Doukhobors' name derives from the Russian term *Doukhobortsi*, spirit-wrestlers. The Russian Orthodox Church, from which the Doukhobors were a break-away sect, regarded them as schismatics wrestling against the Holy Spirit. The sect believed in the cleansing power of fire, and rejected the Bible and the laws of the state. Inevitably they came into conflict with the tsarist regime. After an impassioned campaign by Tolstoy, Quaker leaders, and Aylmer Maude, the Doukhobors were permitted to emigrate from Russia in 1898. Many elected to settle in Canada where most of them were rapidly and peacefully assimilated into the community. Only a tiny and intransigent minority group, styling themselves Sons of Freedom, decided to defy Canadian laws by refusing to register births, marriages and deaths, and by refusing to allow their children to receive public education, or to take the oath of allegiance. They also persisted in the ritual burnings of their Doukhobor homes, and in demonstrating in the nude in accordance with what they believed to be the instructions of God. In her somewhat polemical but informative study of the Sons of Freedom, Simma Holt [60] stresses the extent to which the sect has insulated itself against the influences of Canadian culture. Many are only semi-literate and speak mainly Doukhobor-Russian. Since they do not agree with schooling in government schools because they believe it to be 'corrupting', their children tend to be perpetually disadvantaged in the employment market. Moreover, they have lived in isolated and enclosed communities and have inculcated their children from infancy with Sons of Freedom doctrines. They have taught that they are citizens of the universe, that the only law to be recognised is that of Christ (as interpreted by their leader), and that the government and its laws are of the devil. As their defiance of the Canadian government intensified, so the police and the courts took a tougher line in trying to punish their infractions. In retaliation the Sons of Freedom turned to terroristic violence against the government. They have blown up schools, railways, bridges, power pylons and government buildings, and have caused at least twenty deaths. Holt estimates that between 1924 and 1964 they caused over a thousand depredations and cost the Canadian taxpayers at least twenty million dollars ([60] p. 8). The costs of the sub-revolutionary terrorism waged by even a tiny minority can therefore be quite considerable.

The potential threats and consequences of international terrorism are, however, of a far more serious order. The term international terrorism is of course an ambiguous one. It can mean the exporting of terrorist violence outside the frontiers of the terrorists' state of origin and the killing or injury of foreigners unconnected with the terrorists' struggle. It may also describe the development of international leagues or alliances of terrorists co-ordinating operations on an international scale. As we have noted, neither of these refinements is very new. The I.M.R.O.'s internecine feuds spilt over into Vienna and Milan. Lord Moyne was hunted down in Cairo by the Stern Gang. And in the nineteenth century the Bakuninist International believed it was engaged in an anarchist campaign of European dimensions. What *is* new is the extent to which terrorists have been able to exploit new technological resources in weaponry and communications and publicity. There *has* been a dramatic increase in the incidence of international terrorism. If we examine, for example, the figures on the incidence of the unlawful seizure of aircraft (hijacking) between 1948 and 1970 this increase is clearly shown in Table 2.

It is also interesting that the 'success' rate of hijackers increased between 1971 and 1972, despite the efforts of governments and air lines to find effective counter-measures. In 1971 26 out of 61 attempts succeeded in gaining control of the aircraft.

Table 2

Period	Average Annual Rate of Aircraft Hijacks
1948–58	2·1 aircraft per annum
1958–63	3·3 aircraft per annum
1963–8	7·2 aircraft per annum
1969–70	50·5 aircraft per annum

Source: statistics drawn from *Journal of Air Law & Commerce*, vol. 37 (Spring 1971) pp. 229–33.

In 1972 over half the 72 attempts succeeded, 11 passengers were killed and 14 were injured.

Terrorists have also posed a serious threat to international airports and to grounded aircraft. Three Japanese terrorists working for the Popular Front for the Liberation of Palestine attacked at Lydda Airport on 30 May 1972 and massacred 27 passengers and wounded 71. As *The Economist* observed (3 June 1972), 'The killers were not bargaining for anything. There was virtually no connection between their physical targets and the object of their political disapproval. They were just squirting bullets to produce generalised terror.' The same kind of indiscriminate carnage was meted out to the 32 passengers of the Pan American aircraft at Fiumicino Airport who were killed by terrorist hand grenades thrown into the cabin on 17 December 1973. It is likely that all the terrorists involved in planning and executing these atrocities were youngish, highly educated, and politically fanatical. But according to recent studies of captured hijackers in the United States, not all hijackers are politically motivated. David Hubbard, an American psychiatrist, has concluded that many of them are psychopaths and has described the typical hijacker as a suicidal schizophrenic, frustrated in his private life, excited by violence, and likely to regard the threat of death as a stimulus rather than as a deterrent.

Another technique recently developed and deployed on a large scale by Palestinian terrorists against Jews has been the sending of letter bombs through the international mails. This cowardly form of sowing death and injury is especially tempting to the terrorist as it is difficult to trace the senders of such devices, and letter bombing is a relatively economical and quick operation. One experienced man can pack considerable numbers of letter bombs using small quantities of plastic

123

explosives and miniature detonators. Other methods employed internationally against Jews and Arabs in their war of terrorist dirty tricks have been telephone bombs, shootings, car bombs and the bombing of buildings. Perhaps the most notorious recent shooting was the murder of eleven Israeli athletes and a German policeman in September 1972 at Munich by a Black September group. Palestinian terrorists have also resorted to the seizure of foreign embassies abroad. Having failed to achieve their demands in their seizure of the Israeli Embassy at Bangkok in December 1972 where six hostages were seized, they proceeded to seize the Saudi Arabian Embassy in Khartoum on 1 March 1973. The Khartoum group murdered the American ambassador and his deputy and the Belgian consul-general when terrorist demands for the release of Palestinian prisoners were not met. The record of recent international terrorism is one of murderous lightning striking down the unwary and the innocent.

Two other general conditions conducive to the proliferation of international terrorism need to be borne in mind. There is the fact that many terrorist groups operating overseas are given considerable financial support, weapons, protection and sanctuary by sponsor states, such as Libya. This aid is usefully augmented by help from terrorists' exiled fellow countrymen: for example, Palestinians living in Europe, Croatians in Australia, and Turks in France, have formed useful support communities for international terrorism. The second vital factor is the impact of modern communications media. Terrorists are today given free world-wide publicity: every one of their outrages will be given instant coverage, and where possible journalists and television men will interview the perpetrators and terrorist spokesmen. (This practice raises some important questions about the ethics of news reporting. On occasions when journalists are delivered to some secret rendezvous to interview persons who boast of their part in murder they are, in a sense, aiding and abetting terror. It would be far better if the press and television organisations made a practice of refusing this form of interview. Information on contacts with wanted men should be passed on to the police.) In situations of widespread terrorism a kind of Gresham's Law tends to operate. Extremists

124

will try to outstrip each other in atrocity. They come to believe that those who spill the most blood will make the greatest mark, and they rely absolutely on mass publicity to extract the maximum political advantage from their murders and extortions.

G. PATHOLOGY AND THEORY

Thomas Kuhn has argued that 'later scientific theories are better than earlier ones for solving puzzles in the often quite different environments to which they are applied' ([75] p. 206). He states that the more recent theories can be distinguished from earlier ones by the following criteria: 'accuracy of prediction, particularly of quantitative prediction; the balance between esoteric and everyday subject matter; and the number of different problems solved' ([75] pp. 205–6). Other factors which are less useful but nevertheless important, Kuhn suggests, are scope, simplicity and compatibility with other specialties. Now it must be clearly admitted that in the terms of Kuhn's rigorous criteria there is as yet no adequate and generally accepted scientific theory of political violence or of political terrorism. Much the most valuable insight yielded by modern analysts of political violence belongs to a far older tradition of statecraft and political wisdom, a tradition which it is most foolish to despise. Moss, in his excellent pioneering study of urban guerrillas, illustrates its relevance when he observes: 'many people fail to observe what de Tocqueville pointed out more than a century ago in his classic study of the French Revolution: that, ironically, uprisings often begin at the moment when things are getting better, and there is a genuine possibility of peaceful reform' ([105] p. 16). And it is no reflection on Peter Calvert to note the pure Machiavellianism of some of his generalisations in *A Study of Revolution*: 'Revolutionaries aim to create an impression of power, invincibility and effectiveness, representing themselves as a force which must inevitably assume supremacy. . . . This may not reach the people but it tends to reach government very quickly! . . . a substantial number of governments collapse from internal disillusion and decay . . . because government tries to use the views of the revolutionaries for its own purposes and in so doing rots its own structure' ([15] p. 175). Crozier [27] also forged some propositions about terrorism in a revolutionary context which stand up well to extensive comparative investigation: that terrorism is generally 'the weapon of the weak'; that it is usually a useful auxiliary weapon rather than a decisive one; and that revolutionary terrorism seems to be a strategy most suited to national liberation struggles against foreign rulers, and to use by relatively small conspiratorial movements lacking any power base. Our comparative analysis suggests two further generalisations: first, that terrorism is highly unpredictable in its effects; and second, that terroristic violence can escalate until it is uncontrollable, with terrible results for society.

Nevertheless there are some interesting attempts at a more ambitious general theory, and these will now be examined. One of the most influential is the relative deprivation theory of civil violence, sometimes termed frustration–aggression theory. One of its proponents asserts: 'the necessary precondition for violent civil conflict is relative deprivation, defined as actors' perception of discrepancy between their value expectations and their environment's apparent value capabilities. This deprivation may be individual or collective' ([54] p. 252). There are at least four models of relative deprivation: rising expectations may overtake rising capabilities; capabilities may remain static while expectations rise; general socio-economic malaise may actually bring about a drop in capabilities while expectations remain constant; and finally there is the classic J-curve phenomenon in which, for a period, capabilities keep pace with rising expectations and then suddenly drop behind (a situation identified with the French Revolutionary situation by de Tocqueville). Gurr has elaborated a number of propositions which attempt systematically to relate the level of frustration–aggression (or anger) which is likely to be expressed in civil violence to governmental responses, social control and prevailing ideologies and beliefs. Some of his formal propositions are pitched at such a high level of generality that it is hard to see how they could be invalidated. For example: 'the more intensely people are motivated toward a goal or committed to an attained level of values, the more sharply is interference resented and the greater the consequent instigation to aggression' ([54] p. 257) and 'the strength of anger tends to vary inversely with the extent to which deprivation is held to be legitimate' ([54] p. 260). Gurr also holds that historical traditions and beliefs sanctioning violence, and the absence of institutional mechanisms permitting the expression of non-violent hostility, increase the likelihood and magnitude of civil violence. Of more specific relevance to a theory of terrorism is Gurr's contention that the deprived require 'some congruent image or model of violent action' to trigger them into violence. He suggests that a terrorist act can be used as such a demonstration effect ([54] p. 274).

Yet because of its concentration on frustration–aggression and its 'instinctual' overtones, relative deprivation theory has very little to say about the social psychology of prejudice and hatred and, in particular, about the ways in which such hatreds are learned or acquired. There is widespread agreement in the literature that such hatreds and fanaticisms play a major role in encouraging extreme violence. Contemporary fanaticisms might not evince the monstrous and murderous elements present in the Nazi movement. Nevertheless, racial and religious hatreds have been whipped up in the course of numerous contemporary conflicts; for example in the Middle East, among Northern Irish extremists of both sides and among the Bengalis. As we have noted, there are now ideologues of the extreme left as well as the extreme right who follow Sorel (in [126]) and Fanon in believing collective violence to be creative and cathartic. A more recent development has been the calculated fostering of generational hatreds, a glorification of violence in youth culture. A recent (1972) publication aimed at the 'alternative' or 'underground' movements declares: 'the bombings and the campus riots are not the start of the revolution, they are the defence against an increasing external threat. . . . The bombs of the Angry Brigade and the Weathermen are the result of the constant attempts to destroy it. They are a warning to the death culture. The private property of our parents has become the target for a symbolic vengeance for the lives that have been wantonly destroyed.'[28] A slogan in one illustration in the book

[28] M. Farren, E. Barker *et al.*, *Watch Out Kids* (London: Open Gate Books, 1972).

declares: 'An' when yer smashin' th' state, kids, don't fergit t'keep a smile on yer lips an' a song in yer heart!'

How important is relative deprivation as a determinant of civil violence? Feierabend, Feierabend and Nesvold, in their comparative study of violence covering eighty-four countries, conclude that 'socio-economic frustration' is positively related to conditions of internal political unrest. But they find that it is only one among a number of other important correlates such as a rapid rate of modernisation, the coerciveness of the regime, and the presence of strong minority group populations. Their findings concerning what they term 'systemic conditions of political unrest' are of some interest and are quoted in full:

(a) Political instability is negatively related to indicators of social and economic development.
(b) Political instability is positively related to level of systemic frustration, measured in terms of the ratio (gap) between social wants and social satisfactions within society.
(c) Political instability is positively related to rapid rate of modernization. This relationship holds both for static measures of instability and trends over time.
(d) Political instability is positively related to the level of need achievement within society and especially to increases in need achievement levels between 1925 and 1950.
(e) Political instability is curvilinearly related to level of coerciveness of political regime: the probability of a high level of political instability increases with mid-levels of coerciveness, insufficient to be a deterrent to aggression, but sufficient to increase level of systemic frustration.
(f) Political instability is linearly related to fluctuations in coerciveness of the political regime.
(g) The presence of strong minority populations serves to increase political instability beyond what would be predicted by the fluctuations in coercion.
(h) The higher the level of socioeconomic frustration, the higher the level of coerciveness necessary to act as a deterrent to aggression.

128

(i) The probability of a high level of political instability is greatest with a combination of high levels of socio-economic frustration, high levels of fluctuation in co-erciveness, and mid-level coerciveness of the political regime. ([39] pp. 420–1)

It is a long step, however, from theorising about the conditions for political instability and civil violence in general[29] to a theory of revolutionary terrorism, the subject of the present study. There are at least three main avenues which may provide some progress towards the building of useful theories of revolutionary terrorism. First we can, as several political scientists have urged, concentrate on its essentially *political* pre-conditions, on structures of power and mobilisation processes and their inter-relationship. It is a key premise of this approach that revolutionary violence stems directly from conflicts within and between a country's political institutions. Revolutionary violence is seen as basically the product of conflict about legitimacy, political rights, and access to power. It often results from the refusal or incapacity of a government to meet certain claims made upon it by a powerful group or a coalition of groups.[30] Feliks Gross [51, 52] places primary stress on political factors in his theoretical models of the causation of terror. He has proposed two models; one for the causation of tactical terroristic acts against domestic autocracy or foreign rule, and one for the causation of individual violence as a tactic against democratic institutions.

Gross defines three 'seminal' antecedents for terror against foreign rule or autocracy. The first is a widely perceived condition of oppressive rule, and by oppressive Gross means cruel, brutal, exploitive, arbitrary and humiliating. If the rulers are foreigners then this generally provides an intensification of per-ceived oppression which Gross terms 'sociological' because it 'arises out of ethnic or class subordination or stratification as

29 For a valuable discussion see 'Civil Violence and the International System', Parts I and II, *Adelphi Papers*, nos 82 and 83 (London: International Institute for Strategic Studies, 1971).

30 See [62, 137] for examples of this theoretical approach to revolution.

well as from foreign control . . .' ([52] p. 465). Yet this 'socio-logical' factor is not a sufficient cause of terror. Two other antecedent conditions must exist: an organised group with terroristic tactics and ideology must be available, and there must be activist individuals 'willing to make a political choice and respond with direct action and violence to conditions of oppression' ([52] p. 466). The antecedent conditions for terror against democracy are different. First there must be either an erosion of shared democratic values, a state of anomie, or a crisis of democratic institutions. Secondly, a terroristic organi-sation must exist. Thirdly, there will be a pre-assassination phase directed at subverting and defaming democratic leaders and institutions. And lastly there must be activist personalities prepared to initiate terror. The models are in both cases entirely dependent upon subjective and contingent factors. They should be regarded, as Gross suggests, as no more than useful distillations of causal variables. He suggests an additional general hypothesis of note: assassination and individual terror begin or increase at periods of rising ethnic tensions and ideo-logical–political inequalities rather than as a result of socio-economic strains [51].

Another very influential political hypothesis concerning the causation of terrorism is that put forward by Hannah Arendt ([5] p. 141) suggesting that acts of extreme revolutionary violence in modern states may be a form of desperate revolt against 'rule by Nobody', the anonymity of the bureaucratic state. When Simone Weil castigated the 'bureaucratic machine which excludes all judgement and all genius' and which tends 'to concentrate all powers in itself' ([149] p. 16) she was attacking communist dictatorships. Yet we would surely be justified in taking into account the alienating and atomising effects of all modern highly bureaucratised social systems. Ørvik may be correct in suggesting that the apparently all-pervasive nature of government in post-industrial societies has rendered the insurrection and the *coup d'état* practically obsolete. In these conditions small extremist groups will be tempted to try assassination as an alternative weapon of social change [109]. Crick has pointed out that, 'in an age of bureaucrats, tyrannicide is plainly less useful than terror' ([26] p. 233).

130

The second main line of advance towards a theory of revolutionary terrorism is concentration upon the terrorists themselves; their recruitment and induction into terrorism, their personalities, beliefs and attitudes, and their careers. The invention of revolutionary terrorism implies the invention of a new profession, the professional terrorist. One of the most thorough-going explorations of the terrorist in modern literature is that of Malraux in his novel *La Condition humaine* [94]. Konig, the repressive police chief serving Chiang Kai-shek in Shanghai in early 1927, is portrayed as a man seeking to erase the memory of his own humiliation at the hands of the Russians by wholesale murder and torture: 'My dignity is to kill them.' But even this is not enough; he feels driven to humiliate his victims before their death, just as he was humiliated by his Russian captors. Malraux's archetypal revolutionary terrorist is portrayed in the character of Ch'en, a westernised young Chinese who creates his own personal ideology of terrorism. Malraux suggests that Ch'en resorts to professional terror to escape from his private anguish, his extreme loneliness, and the fact that he needs to serve a cause and yet lacks faith in anything except his own power to destroy. Though he begins his terrorist career by murdering a sleeping man as an act of revolutionary duty, the political motives or purposes of his acts become increasingly irrelevant for him. Ch'en becomes consumed by terrorism as an end in itself. He can only forget himself by becoming a lonely executioner and sacrificing his own life: 'Il fallait que le terrorisme devint une mystique. Solitude, d'abord: que le terroriste décidât seul, exécutât seul; . . .' ([94] p. 189). In his famous play, *Les Justes* [16], Camus distinguishes between the cynically opportunist terrorist (represented by Stepan) and the genuinely idealist revolutionary (Kaliaev) who believes that an act of assassination may be justified in the furtherance of the revolutionary crusade. In presenting the clash of these two attitudes to revolutionary action, Camus implies that there must be clearly defined *limits* to violence, limits that we transgress at our peril. Kaliaev, the revolutionary idealist, comes to believe that it is only permissible to kill in furtherance of 'the cause' provided the terrorist is prepared to sacrifice his own life. But is this convincing? Does

131

a terrorist's self-immolation in some way extenuate his taking another's life?

Marx is quite candid about the strange bedfellows that accompany every revolution: 'In every revolution there intrude at the side of its true agents, men of a different stamp; some of them survivors of, and devotees to, past revolutions without insight into the present movement, but preserving popular influence by their honesty and courage or by the sheer force of tradition, others mere brawlers . . .' ([97] p. 67). We should be warned against any crude attempts to stereotype terrorists. There is much evidence to support the view that some revolutionaries are impelled by passionate idealism and conviction. As one authority on anarchism observes, 'for many anarchists, the belief in education, co-operation and peaceful persuasion goes hand in hand with a belief in direct action and even with active involvement in schemes for assassination' ([66] p. 214), and he cites the case of the Spanish educationalist Francisco Ferrer in illustration. Nor should we assume that political terrorism is the pursuit of the less intelligent or less able. On the contrary, there is considerable evidence that revolutionary terrorism attracts the highly educated, and that the university student body is one of its major sources of recruitment. Dr David Hubbard's portrait of the typical American hijacker as a suicidal schizophrenic with criminal or psychopathic tendencies *may* have some practical use as the basis for a crude 'hijacker profile' for use by security officers at U.S. airports. But as it is aimed at the criminal or psychopathic hijacker it is of no use in identifying the explicitly political terrorist. Thus, for example, the Japanese who perpetrated the massacre at Lydda Airport were hardly noticed when they boarded the aircraft at Rome and their luggage in the hold was not searched. And indeed on what evidence could the authorities have suspected them? Far more questionable is a recent attempt to stereotype terrorists as 'sociopaths' using the Wechsler intelligence measurement scales (see [122]). There is not a shred of evidence to substantiate the claim that political terrorists are below average in abstract thinking: indeed it could be argued that with many terrorists the reverse is the case; they are prepared to sacrifice all humane considerations and often their lives for the sake of abstractions. Nor is it proven that terrorists are educationally retarded.

Political terrorism cannot be understood outside the context of the development of terroristic, or potentially terroristic, ideologies, beliefs and life-styles. Most influential has been the tradition of romantic individualism developed by Goethe, Humboldt, Schiller and Stefan George in Germany. They posited a heroic genius forced into conflict with society or into isolation by the philistinism of the world. Max Stirner elaborated this individualism into a cult of the self-assertive egoist which in its amorality and anti-intellectualism anticipated certain currents in modern existentialism [130]. The existentialist idea, so powerfully articulated by Camus and Sartre, that it is only through our own *actions* or *acts of will* that we can escape from despair, has been enormously pervasive. Under certain conditions such beliefs can become powerfully conducive to acts of terrorism. They can create a kind of politics of will and glorification of action for its own sake of the kind which Marinetti and the Futurists expounded. In the age of industrial organisations, machines, and mass armies, extremists of Left and Right may come to feel that all effective forms of symbolic action are exhausted. They may become convinced that acts of terrorism are the only means of asserting individual will and power. The culmination of this politics of the blood is an utterly amoral aestheticisation of politics: 'Qu'importe les victimes, si le geste est beau?'[31] The fact is that for some, though by no means all, terrorists extreme violence is primarily undertaken as an act of self-assertion and self-expression. Paradoxically, therefore, acts of terrorism which occur as acts of will (though often given a post-facto political rationalisation by others) are not truly political; they are anti-political.

It is this writer's view that the psychology and beliefs of terrorists have been inadequately explored to date, although such a study could be a valuable aid to advance in the subject. Much more influential, yet disappointingly fruitless, has been the third avenue of approach via military and insurgency theory. Although, as we have noted, the French have evolved

[31] Words of Laurent Tailhade on hearing that an anarchist bomb had been thrown in the Chamber of Deputies.

a military doctrine of revolutionary power, and although 'insurgency studies' have had a certain vogue in American social science, remarkably little of the literature on guerrilla war and insurgency contributes directly to a theory of terrorism. The most influential theoretical model of the role of revolutionary terrorism in internal war is Thornton's [136]. Following Crozier [27] Thornton accepts that terrorism is normally associated with the initial phase of internal war, that is as a preliminary to full-scale guerrilla operations. But Thornton's model is sufficiently flexible to allow for the fact that terror can be employed simultaneously with guerrilla and conventional war phases. His model of the role of insurgent and incumbent terror at the various phases of internal war is summarised in Table 3 below.

Table 3

Phase	Insurgents		Incumbents		Totals
	Agitational	Enforcement	Enforcement	Agitational	
Preparatory	0	0	Low	0	Low
Initial violence	High	Low	High	0	High
Expansion	Intermediate	Intermediate	Low	Low	High
Victorious	Low	High	0	Low	Intermediate
Consolidation	0	0	0	0	0

Source: Thornton [136] pp. 92–5.

In his exposition of the consolidation phase Thornton does concede that the new incumbents will generally use 'a considerable degree' of enforcement terror, but argues that this is not connected with the internal war situation. He argues that terror generally reaches its maximum in the initial stage when 'the incumbents, if they have not previously detected the movement, must now launch their maximum enforcement attack if they hope to stifle the movement. At this stage, therefore, both agitational and enforcement terrors will be at a maximum' ([136] p. 93). The deficiencies of Thornton's model as the basis for a theory of terrorism are quite obvious. In fairness, Thornton does not make ambitious claims for the model. It is clearly only appropriate in certain archetypal internal war situations and does not really fit the many cases of struggles waged almost entirely by means of terrorism. Many of these, as we have observed, simply do not conform to the phasing of the model. Thornton does not offer any purchase on problems of terrorist motivation, or for identifying the conditions conducive to the adoption of revolutionary terrorism.

A surprising lacuna in strategic studies of revolutionary terrorism is the absence of a full treatment of weapon availability and supply and of the implications of new weapon technology for terrorism. Sir Frank Blackaby, at the British Association meeting (general section) in 1972, hinted at the nightmare possibility of a terrorist group seizing control over a nuclear device and attempting to blackmail government and society. So far these weapons have been successfully monopolised by states: the rapid proliferation of nuclear expertise and the recently announced American development of a 'pocket' nuclear weapon device make this threat considerably more credible. Practically every other kind of weapon, short of nuclear, is potentially obtainable from the arms dealers or from sympathetic or neutral states. Peter Calvert comments interestingly on the effects of the technical improvement of weapons which enable persons to kill one another at relatively greater distances. He suggests that this increase in distance is sufficient to prevent the aggressive instinct of the user from being controlled by the normal restraints of face-to-face fighting. Calvert observes, 'though this gives advantage to the defence where forces are evenly matched, it also enables one deviant to kill a very large number of people single-handed' ([15] p. 176). The case of Villain, Jaurès's assassin, would suggest the truth of this claim. Villain confessed that he had been unable to go through with his first attempt at assassination because of the look of goodness and serenity he saw in his victim's eyes. Is the intensification of terror directly related to the physical distance of the terrorist fighter from his target?

4. Counter-measures

We should shed no tears for tyrants or brutal and repressive rulers who are confronted by revolutionary terrorism: they reap the whirlwind of their own terror. In such regimes it is justifiable, however, to ask to what extent the innocent are likely to suffer by the revolutionaries' terror, and whether the revolutionary movement has any reasonable chance of success. As we have noted, by definition totalitarian regimes suppress all effective opposition within their boundaries and are entirely unimpeded by any judicial or humanitarian constraints. The present writer has remarked elsewhere: 'the sacrifice and heroic courage of those who rose in the Warsaw Ghetto against the Nazis was tragic proof that even the most determined and desperate attempt by an urban-based liberation movement could not hold out against the superior technology and firing power of a ruthless occupying force which was prepared to liquidate all who stood in its way' ([151] p. 138). Rural-based movements in ideal terrain stand a rather better chance of survival. But for autocracies and totalitarian regimes the only 'problems' of counter-measures against terrorism are those concerned with secret police or military techniques.

Domestic revolutionary terrorism does create serious problems for liberal democracies. The liberties of a democratic society are ultimately dependent upon the maintenance of the rule of law. Individual rights and protection from arbitrary rule have to be preserved by a judiciary which is seen not only to be independent and impartial but also *effective*. Legal sanctions must be seen to be implemented. Unless government ensures that the law of the land is obeyed, the whole system of rights and obligations breaks down. If the law and constitution of the land come to be openly and regularly defied and held in contempt, the rule of law will collapse and every man will become judge in his own cause. In the ensuing Hobbesian struggle of all against all, the strongest individuals would be free to tyrannise the weak. Terrorism is the most flagrant form of defiance of the rule of law. It challenges government's prerogative of the monopoly of armed force within the state. Terrorists attempt to replace the laws of the state by their own law of the gun and the kangaroo court. It is therefore vital for government to act speedily and forcefully against them and, above all, to preserve their power to govern. Nor will any humane government be prepared to tolerate the appalling social and economic casualties and damage which, as we have earlier observed, inevitably result from terrorist operations.

It cannot be sufficiently emphasised that terrorists in liberal democracies are *making war* on the lawful popularly elected government. In the face of gun and bomb it would be as foolish to argue with them as it would be to present a protest note to an invading army. Government must prove that it can meet such threats with force. But past lessons of terrorist campaigns show that it would be wise to bear in mind certain fundamental ground rules. Government must not be seen to give in to terrorist blackmail or intimidation. This would weaken the position of the moderates, and also encourage the revolutionaries to use terrorism to gain further demands. The authorities must also convince the general population that they can protect them against the terrorists: otherwise the terrorists will use coercive terror on the population to compensate for any lack of support. Moreover, if the legal order is seen to have broken down, para-military 'self-defence' groups will proliferate, and feud violence, vengeance murders, and a general crime wave, are likely to result. Above all the government must seek to avoid alienating the support of the mass of the population. As Moss [105] rightly emphasises, it is the terrorists' intention to provoke a campaign of governmental repression which will turn the people against the government. Hence, to needlessly harass, frighten, or in any way harm the general population, is to play into the hands of the terrorists and to present them with potential recruits and sympathisers. Thus, while government is dealing effectively with the military and security threat posed by the terrorists, it must also be engaged in a political struggle with the political wing of the terrorist movement to win the allegiance of the people. Experience of past terrorist struggles indicates that the government cannot win unless it energetically produces reforms to meet the major grievances or demands of the citizens. This combination of strong security measures and social reform is sometimes termed the 'two wars' strategy.

The cardinal aim of this strategy is to isolate the terrorists from their host population. It is a politically constructive approach because it combines long-term prophylactic measures with immediate action to contain and reduce the level of violence. But it is a strategy fraught with risks and requiring an extraordinarily high degree of skill, determination and patience on the part of government and security forces. We have noted in an earlier chapter the evidence that high levels of civil violence tend to occur at mid-levels of coerciveness by the regime: it is precisely at these levels that the two-war strategy must operate. Government must achieve the almost super-human task of using enough force to deter terrorist aggression while at the same time avoiding any damage or injury to the innocent whose moral support and co-operation they require. If the government uses excessive repression it will not only alienate popular support and incline the people to listen to the revolutionaries; it will turn itself into a despotism. The history of the Russian judicial reforms of 1864 is instructive in this connection. Liberals rejoiced at the promise of these measures: a permanent and independent judiciary was established for the first time in Russia; trial by jury for all serious criminal cases was instituted; the old class courts (except the *volost* or peasant courts) were scrapped; and all trials were to be held in public. Yet by the end of the century these great advances had been undermined: the Minister of Justice had gained power to dis-miss judges at will; right of jury trial was withdrawn in an increasing number of cases; courts with 'class representatives' were again resorted to, and the authorities acquired powers to order trials *in camera* for a wide range of cases. Civilians became subject to trial by courts-martial and the authorities gained power to exile without trial. Government was thus placed beyond the reach of the law. As Laurence Housman remarked, in the context of decree rule in pre-war India, such arbitrary

138

methods are 'a terror to innocent and guilty alike; and where they fail to terrorise, they provoke and rouse to acts of resistance thousands who would not have resisted a process of law which they saw to be just . . .' ([61] p. 6).

On the other hand, if the government is too soft with terrorists, if it is too ready to make concessions, the terrorists will be encouraged to increase their demands, and other extremist groups will be encouraged to resort to terrorist blackmail. The ground will be cut from beneath the feet of law-abiding moderates, and the government's own authority will be gravely undermined. An extreme example of government conceding too much too quickly was in the British government's handling of the terrorist campaign in Aden. The government announced in 1966 that it would pull all its forces out of Aden in 1968 whatever internal security conditions might prevail at that time. As Paget remarks, the security forces lost all hope of local co-operation from that moment on ([110] p. 159). In order to maintain the morale of the security forces, and public confidence in the government it is essential that the government should make clear its intention to maintain its authority and to implement its policies. It would, however, be rather foolhardy to do as one military analyst has suggested, and announce that it is going to 'destroy the subversive movement utterly' ([72] p. 50). In the first place this is to set itself what is generally an unattainable aim. Secondly, such a position robs the government of any flexibility of political manoeuvre or of any possibility of peacefully assimilating the rebel elements into the polity by negotiation. Another very serious error to be avoided is violent fluctuation in the amount of coercion used by government. We have noted earlier the positive correlation between such fluctuation and high levels of civil violence. The public will only become bewildered by such swings in government response, while the terrorists will be encouraged into believing that the government's counsels are divided (probably this *will* be the case in any democratic regime) and will try to exploit and widen differences within government. Obvious vacillation by government will be interpreted as weakness.

Having considered the general ground-rules for anti-terrorist action we must now examine some of the measures and

139

methods that have either been tried or proposed for use against terrorism. At the political level special or emergency powers acts have been useful for various purposes. They may be used to proscribe membership in, or support of, terrorist organisations, and to forbid the raising of private armies and the wearing of para-military uniforms. The clandestine core of the terrorist organisation will not be hindered, but such measures, will help the government by preventing the terrorists' political wing from making a display of political strength. Such measures should be combined with proscription of marches and demonstrations. This will help to reduce the burden of the security forces for whom inter-movement street-fighting is an especially serious worry. Another particularly useful set of measures are those designed to regulate the registration of fire-arms, the availability and use of explosives, and the sale of potentially dangerous chemicals and weapons. The most cogent argument in favour of laws restricting private ownership of guns is that fire-arms are more often lethal than other readily available weapons (such as knives). If guns are not widely available, those who commit acts of violence, but who do not have a single-minded desire to murder, are less likely to kill [157]. The only means of counteracting the build-up of illegal arms is, however, thorough and constant arms searching by the security forces, including, of course, the use of naval and air patrols to prevent arms smuggling.

The most difficult and controversial problems of special powers acts are concerned with the treatment of captured terrorists, or of those suspected of belonging to, or of aiding or abetting, a terrorist organisation. Security forces argue strongly for the power to hold suspects without trial as an emergency measure. Many police and military spokesmen are in favour of suspension of habeas corpus and powers of internment on two main grounds. One is that there is not always sufficient evidence available to secure conviction of the terrorist in a court of law. The other more weighty argument is that normal processes of law cannot function properly in a terrorist conflict. Juries, witnesses and lawyers and their families are often intimidated, and for this reason trial by jury for offences under the emergency powers acts is often suspended. Now it is but a short step from the development of sweeping special powers such as these to the institution of martial law. No democratic government worth the name would deserve continuing public support if it went over to military rule for any length of time. Therefore constant efforts must be made to ensure that any special powers measures of the kind described are combined with full and impartial procedures of appeal and judicial review. One of the most disastrous political consequences of military-decree rule is that by summary executions and punishments (of the kind meted out in Dublin in 1916) new martyrs and new holy wars are born.

Should the army be given the major security role in terrorist situations? Kitson [72] is quite adamant that in the United Kingdom the army has 'the obligation for maintaining law and order' ([72] p. 24). Many in government and in the army do not accept this view. They argue that for the last hundred years or so this responsibility has been delegated to the civil police, that the police forces have generally proved quite adequate for the tasks involved, and that it is right and necessary for the police, given constant improvement of their resources and skills, to continue to do the job. Kitson is himself convinced of the need for full civil–military co-ordination and accepts the need for government to scrutinise military proposals to 'ensure that they do not cut across long-term government aims' ([72] p. 52). But his insistence on 'unified planning, centralized control and a single point of responsibility' (p. 53) does clearly imply some form of military rule, albeit temporary. He argues that the army is specially qualified to combat subversion, to build up the vital intelligence network necessary to combat terrorists, and to conduct psychological warfare operations. All this sounds remarkably like a British variant of French army doctrine on revolutionary warfare, and it is worth recalling our finding that this French military exercise was marked by *political* failure.

There are clearly some tasks for which the army is uniquely fitted by its professional experience and expertise. For example, its superb corps of bomb-disposal specialists, and troops specially trained to use image-intensifying sights at night, are invaluable in anti-terrorist operations. But there is no reason to assume that the vital tasks of security patrolling and the gathering of intelligence are beyond the capabilities of a well-trained, well-led, and adequately rewarded police service. There are, moreover, very considerable disadvantages attached to prolonged use of the army as an anti-terrorist force. The objections of cost and the undue strain placed on our already inadequate service manpower are well known. It is also obvious that such operations involve the employment of highly trained technician personnel in garrison-type duties: there simply are insufficient infantry available to do the job. Security duties in a modern city may have extremely corrosive effects on military morale, because of long, tedious patrol duties and the constraints on full-scale military response to sniping and attack. What is not so often realised is that prolonged use of the army in a security role can in itself exacerbate social divisions, even though the army may make heroic efforts to avoid this. The use of soldiers who are essentially strangers drafted into the locality to do an unenviable job, and who mostly live in quarters inevitably separated from the population, is bound to provoke resentment and hostility. Hostility easily spills over into aggression when, however infrequently, the soldiers make mistakes and harm the innocent. As Charles Douglas-Home has perceptively observed: 'The effect is to elevate into a full-scale war, movements that are basically on a much smaller scale. . . . the trouble with insurgencies is that they can only be countered so far with war-by-wallchart. . . . the danger of this approach is that it imposes a permanent military dimension on the area which raises communal violence to a more permanent and formal level.'[32]

One positive recommendation made by Harold Wilson in September 1972 deserves serious consideration not only by the British government but also by other liberal democracies. He has proposed the formation of a specially trained anti-terrorist section with the special skills and resources required. Mr Wilson's suggestion is that such a unit could be formed from an appropriate section of the army. For reasons stated in the foregoing discussion the writer is of the view that an anti-terrorist squad should be formed within the police structure and that it

[32] Article in *The Times*, 19 December 1973.

should draw its key officers from the existing Special Branch. It must be generously endowed with research facilities, and it must be armed. It should be able to operate nation-wide, and should be directly responsible to the Home Secretary.

MEASURES AGAINST INTERNATIONAL TERRORISM

There are no simple solutions to the problems posed by the internationalisation of revolutionary terrorism, just as there are no easy answers to the problems of preventing war terror or the repressive terror of states. In the case of repressive terror there is an appalling gulf between the rhetoric of charters of human rights and the actual processes of law and punishment in states (see [1]). The Nuremberg War Crimes Tribunals declared that the murder of non-combatants, and the killing of hostages were crimes against humanity. Article 39 of the 1949 Geneva Convention outlaws the collective punishment of communities for acts by individuals for which they were not collectively responsible. But how often are governments and their military brought to account for such crimes? Predictably, most of those brought to trial for war crimes have been in the service of defeated powers, and have been arraigned before the victors' courts.

The principles of state sovereignty and of non-intervention in the internal affairs of other states are deeply embedded in the Westphalian normative system of international relations. National governments have at their disposal concentrations of armed force which are overwhelmingly superior to those which movements can muster. International terrorists have no recognised status in international law: they are regarded as *francs-tireurs*, and when they are captured governments may dispose of them as they wish. The conditions laid down by the Hague Convention for the recognition of guerrillas as lawful belligerents are so tightly drawn that in practice they do not cover the international political terrorist. Under Article 1 they would, in order to qualify for lawful belligerent status, need to be in the service of a *de jure* or *de facto* government (including, possibly, the case of a revolutionary government in power over a base area). And, among other conditions, they are required to carry arms openly and to conduct their operations in accordance with

143

the laws and customs of war. As for those terrorists whose motive is to plunder, they are regarded in international law as pirates, *hostes humani generis*. Any governments into whose hands they fall may do with them as they will: pirates are deprived of the protection of their own state of origin.

How is it that international terrorists, faced by the superior forces and legal powers of the state, have come to be regarded as a dangerous threat to the community of states? Some would argue that the damage they have done to lives and property is a pinprick compared to the destruction wrought by warring states. It would be reasonable to assume that the appetite of the news media for reporting sensational atrocities has helped to create a wildly exaggerated view of the importance of terrorist actions. One international-relations scholar has remarked, 'it can be argued that they (the terrorists) have so far done no more than create a series of nuisances for the international order' ([14] p. 31). Yet there are considerable grounds for judging this to be a short-sighted assessment. Terrorist movements using violence independently against a state with which they are in direct conflict, or against the citizens or officials of third-party states, tend to embroil states in international disputes and conflicts and thus to generally exacerbate international differences. They may bring about sufficient disruption within a particular state to provoke a redeployment of forces for internal security, and they may thus affect local and central power balances. International terrorist techniques will tend to be emulated if they are seen to bring quick rewards, as has been the case with hijacking of aircraft and kidnapping. If extortion and blackmail techniques are seen to pay then inevitably, as Moss [105] rightly emphasises, the terrorists' demands will escalate. Terrorists forced the Brazilian government to release fifteen prisoners in return for the release of the U.S. ambassador held hostage. To obtain the release of the West German ambassador the price was forty prisoners, while for the Swiss ambassador it reached seventy. Nor should we neglect the human and social costs of terrorist action. The total number of kidnapped or hijacked hostages killed or injured may be relatively small compared to the casualties of internal war. The grief of those bereaved by such outrages is just as real. Western governments, with their relatively open and mobile societies and their complex communications systems, *are* increasingly vulnerable to international terrorist attack: it is widely recognised that some kind of swift and effective measures must be taken to reduce this vulnerability.

In earlier comparative discussion of revolutionary terrorist movements it has been noted that certain states in the past have helped to initiate and sustain the activities of terrorist movements within states to which they were opposed. (For example Germany and Italy in the 1930s were heavily implicated in a number of Balkan terrorist movements.) This method of waging a terrorist war by proxy is proving still more attractive to many governments in the conditions of the nuclear 'balance of terror'. Many contemporary regimes of varying ideological hues are engaged in a kind of complex secret war of movements, and are expending considerable sums on arming and training them for terrorist activities. Major centres for this 'sponsored' relationship have been Algiers, Libya, Damascus, Peking, Hanoi, Dar-es-Salaam, Zaire and Havana. Indeed it is evident that those movements that do not enjoy the benefits of such sponsorship (such as the Basques, the Breton nationalists, and the Kurds) really cannot compete in big-league international terrorist operations which require considerable resources and the sanctuary of a friendly state. A second significant recent trend has been the burgeoning of international collaboration between terrorist movements with quite different political goals. There has been bilateral co-operation between the I.R.A. and the Basque separatists, between the Palestinian and Turkish liberation movements, and even more unpredictably, between Japanese revolutionaries and the Popular Front for the Liberation of Palestine. At a recent conference for an Arab front to support the Palestine resistance movement (held in Beirut), delegations from the Tupamaros, Vietcong, and other revolutionary movements are reported to have attended.[33] In addition regional movement blocs have developed such as the Organisation of Latin American Solidarity, and the Liberation Committee of the Organisation of African Unity. Though often rent by schisms they do provide a machinery for co-ordinating

[33] Report in *The Times*, 30 November 1972.

activities. It would certainly be mistaken to assume, in the face of all the evidence of collaboration, that most terrorist groups today remain self-reliant in weaponry and organisation.[34]

These background conditions must be borne in mind if one is to fully understand the reasons for the intractability of the problems of combating international terrorism. It would be clearly foolish to underestimate the energy, resourcefulness, and ruthless cunning of the terrorist groups and sponsor states involved. At the same time it must be stressed that much of the dedicated support given to the dangerous (and sometimes suicidal) international terrorist missions stems from conviction, anger, hatred and despair. Political terrorism, as suggested earlier, is not necessarily the work of psychopaths, even though one may regard it as an especially loathsome weapon. To understand why large numbers of Palestinians, for example, openly rejoice in each new terrorist 'success' is to understand the roots of their feelings of anger and bitter humiliation. They believe they were robbed of their homeland by a new Jewish state which most of them still refuse to recognise as legitimate, and which many of them are deeply committed to destroying. Set in its proper historical context, therefore, much of the recent wave of international terrorism can be best understood not as the establishment of a permanent pattern of violence, but as a violent and desperate aftermath of the Arab defeat in the 1967 War.

One must not forget also that the socio-psychological impact of modern war long survives the formal ending of hostilities. Whole town and village communities may suffer decimation or expulsion from their homes. Many families are forced to become permanent exiles or refugees. Deep bitterness between the peoples of nations formerly at war can poison international relations. The generations who have fought in, or have lived through, war are hardened by the conditions of war, inured to the facts of terror and the cheapness of human life. Those mobilised into military service will, in addition, have acquired an expertise in weaponry and military organisation which they may then utilise as members of guerrilla revolutionary or counter-revolutionary forces. These conditions are conducive to

[34] See Moss [105] for a statement of the contrary view.

a reintroduction of terror when this appears to offer tempting gains in a political conflict.

The political consequences may be so disastrous as to virtually ensure a recrudescence of war and terror as soon as forces are regrouped and re-equipped. Between November 1947, when the U.N. voted for partition of Palestine, and May 1948 when Britain withdrew, some three hundred thousand Arabs became refugees. (The Arabs claim this was under duress from the Israeli forces. Israel denies this.) After the proclamation of the state of Israel, over four hundred thousand further refugees fled into neighbouring Arab states in the course of the fighting. Each new phase of the war has added to the refugee problem. In a recent study of the Palestinian refugee situation, Gerald Blake claims: 'The Six-Day War was a cataclysm for the Palestinians, for it demonstrated that the restoration of Palestine could not be achieved by the Arab armies. The Palestine movement received a new lease of life. Old organizations received numerous recruits and several dozen new movements sprang up with the aim of overthrowing Israel by whatever means' ([11] p. 180). After the efforts of Hussein to crush the *fedayeen*, new methods and organisations were developed. One of these is Black September. This experience provides a graphic illustration of the direct relationship between the effects of war, changes of frontiers, displacement of persons, and the inauguration of terroristic response. It is a hopeful possibility that one of the consequences of any lasting settlement of Arab grievances in the Middle East would be a decline in the incidence of international terrorism.

The underlying causes of international terrorism are to a large extent to be found in political, social and economic problems that have defied attempts to resolve them by national governments, regional organisations and the United Nations. We cannot look to any international authority for a magic formula to eliminate terrorism. Past attempts at international action have been largely futile. Russia tried to achieve an international treaty obligating signatory states to extradite political terrorists for political murder. (This effort followed Alexander II's assassination in 1881.) They failed. The 1937 League of Nations treaty making extradition or prosecution of political

147

terrorists mandatory was signed by twenty-three states. But those states actively promoting terror in the 1930s did not sign and the treaty was as worthless as the Kellogg Pact. In its recent debates on the subject, the United Nations General Assembly has shown itself totally divided. Predictably the governments urging tough action have included Israel, South Africa and Portugal. The main African, Arab and Asian bloc of new states has resolutely opposed both discussion and international action on the subject on the grounds that action might be directed against the various liberation movements which they champion. The British and the Russians supported an American proposal for an international convention on the problem of terrorism. The Chinese delegate reflected a widely held Afro-Asian view in his speech opposing the proposal. He argued that matters concerning terrorism should be handled by countries in which terrorist acts occurred. The Chinese were opposed to 'adventurist' actions, he claimed, but they were also against allowing 'imperialism' to use terrorist incidents to villify and suppress national liberation struggles. Any discussion of terrorism should include consideration of imperialist and other forms of aggression.[35] In December 1972 the U.N. General Assembly voted to establish a Study Committee to examine terrorism. This proposal was incorporated in a resolution condemning 'the continuation of repressive and terrorist acts by colonial, racist and alien regimes'.[36] There are few grounds for hope that any effective United Nations action will emerge from this committee. International meetings of this kind serve to reflect the self-interest of the participants and are used as a platform for propaganda. United Nations debates do provide a means by which states sympathetic to terrorist movements can show their colours and reveal at least some of the motives underlying such support.

The Hague and Montreal Conventions on the unlawful seizure of aircraft provide classic examples of the ineffectuality of world bodies in combating terrorism. The Hague Convention of December 1970 laid down rules to bind all signatories to the extradition or prosecution of hijackers. So far only one-third of

[35] *Proceedings of the General Assembly*, 22 November 1972.
[36] *Proceedings of the General Assembly*, 19 December 1972.

the governments belonging to the International Civil Aviation Organisation have ratified it. This is not enough to make it effective. Even if states such as Algeria, Syria and Libya, which have readily provided sanctuary for hijackers, were pressured into signing the Convention, they would be able to circumvent it by meting out only token punishments. The Montreal Convention of 1971 attempted to frame rules that would give the I.C.A.O. real 'teeth' to act against offending governments by adding provision for collective sanctions against countries harbouring terrorists. By the end of 1973 less than a dozen countries had ratified the Montreal Convention.[37]

There is one sensible conclusion to be drawn from these sad stories of frustrated hopes. The best hope for effective action to reduce the vulnerability of liberal democracies to attacks by international terrorists lies in the adoption of stronger anti-terrorist measures by individual governments, and in the formulation of a European Community policy against terrorism. For all members of the European Community have a common interest in preserving their way of life, their civil peace, and their increasingly integrated economic and communications system, against terrorism. For a number of reasons western Europe is a sitting target for Arab terrorism: it is in close geographical proximity to the Arab world; there are large immigrant worker populations, including many Arabs, living in most of the major cities; these immigrants are often discriminated against in economic and social policies and they therefore more readily support extremist fellow-countrymen; many Europeans, both Jewish and non-Jewish, are sympathetic towards Israel, and European countries have aided Israel both militarily and economically; nor should we neglect the residual anti-European feeling among the Arabs left over from the days of direct colonial rule. Arab terrorists have frequently indicated that all western European states are their targets: typical of such threats is a recent statement by a spokesman for the Eagles of the Palestinian Revolution (E.P.R.) who claimed, 'we have a chain of well-trained underground cells complete with sophisticated

[37] See McWhinney [89, 90] for a comprehensive analysis of the problems involved in the development of international law on hijacking.

equipment in every European country ready to strike any time, anywhere in the continent.'[38]

There are a number of measures that the European Community could introduce in order to increase the security of its citizens and governments. *The Economist*, the journal which has provided by far the ablest reporting and analysis on the subject of terrorism, suggested some of the most useful short-term measures in a recent article.[39] There should be tighter airport movement controls, closer passport and immigration vetting, and the West German measure requiring entry visas from Libyans, Moroccans, and Tunisians as well as citizens of other Arab states should be seriously considered by other European countries. There should be more extensive surveillance of exile political groups in western Europe, and the proscription of foreign extremist organisations known or suspected to be terrorist should be considered. One vital need, in the writer's view, is for greater centralised co-ordination of anti-terrorist police investigation and counter-measures. It is at present all too easy for terrorists to confuse each national police force by moving their operations rapidly from one European centre to another. Interpol is quite unfitted for the task as its rules preclude it from dealing with politically motivated crime. What is required is a European Community anti-terrorist group to work under the direction of the Council of Ministers. These proposed measures are radical and potentially costly. But the risks involved demand forceful action, and these measures, in combination, would have the wider advantage of helping to inhibit hijacking and kidnapping activities in the world community.

Inaction or inadequate action against terrorists is a recipe for disaster. This is well illustrated in the unhappy experience of Australia in dealing with Ustashi terrorists based within her borders. Some Australian political leaders chose to turn a blind eye to the growth of Croatian terrorist training camps and organisations. Some actively backed the Ustashi because they were anti-Communists. In a bomb explosion in the Yugoslav Travel Agency in Sydney in September 1972, fifteen people

[38] Report in *The Times*, 4 October 1973.

[39] 'The Anti-Terrorists', *The Economist*, 16 September 1972, pp. 15–18.

were injured. The Yugoslav government threatened to break off diplomatic relations and the Australian government had a first-class international dispute on its hands. Another illustration of governmental weakness in the face of international terrorism was the Austrian government's promise in September 1973 to close the transit camps for Soviet Jews emigrating to Israel. The Austrian Chancellor made this promise in response to the threats of a Black September group who had hijacked a trainload of Soviet Jews and threatened to kill their hostages if their demands were not met. The Israeli government had urged strongly that the Austrians should not give in to the terrorists. It was certain that the surrender would eliminate an invaluable escape route for Soviet Jews and probable that such a coup would tempt terrorists to make still more outrageous demands in their future operations.

The guiding principle of a European anti-terrorist policy must be never to surrender to blackmail or extortion. Terrorists will only abandon kidnapping hostages or hijacking passengers if they discover that governments refuse to grant their demands. Searches, the use of armed guards, a counter-attack or a ruse to defeat the terrorists – these are sensible alternative responses to threats by terrorists and hijackers. Governments must aim to combat terrorism and win. And to this end the governments of Europe will find strength through unity.

Bibliography

Wherever possible English language sources and the most recent editions of works are given.

[1]   Amnesty International, *Report on Torture* (London: Duckworth, 1973).

[2]   Hannah Arendt, *On Revolution* (London: Faber & Faber, 1964).

[3]   Hannah Arendt, *Eichmann in Jerusalem: A Report on the Banality of Evil*, revised and enlarged edn (New York: Viking Press, 1965).

[4]   Hannah Arendt, *The Origins of Totalitarianism*, 3rd edn (London: Allen & Unwin, 1967).

[5]   Hannah Arendt, 'On Violence' in *Crises of the Republic*, (Harmondsworth: Penguin, 1973) pp. 83-163.

[6]   Raymond Aron, *Peace and War* (London: Weidenfeld & Nicolson, 1966).

[7]   St Augustine, *The City of God*, ed. and intro. by Vernon J. Bourke (New York: Image Books, 1958).

[8]   Paul Avrich, *The Russian Anarchists* (Princeton University Press, 1967).

[9]   Tom Barry, *Guerilla Days in Ireland* (Tralee: Anvil Books, 1968).

[10] Menachem Begin, *The Revolt* (New York: Henry Schuman, 1951).

[11] Gerald Blake, 'The Wandering Arabs', *Geographical Magazine*, 45, 3 (December 1972) pp. 179–82.

[12] Paul Bohannan, *Social Anthropology* (New York: Holt, Rinehart, & Winston, 1963).

[13] David Boulton, *The U.V.F. 1966–1973*, Torc Books (Dublin: Gill & Macmillan, 1973).

[14] Hedley Bull, 'Civil Violence and International Order', *Adelphi Papers No. 83*, Part II (London: International Institute for Strategic Studies, 1971) pp. 27–36.

[15] Peter Calvert, *A Study of Revolution* (Oxford: Clarendon Press, 1970).

[16] Albert Camus, *The Just*, in *Collected Plays*, trans. Stuart Gilbert (London: Hamish Hamilton, 1965).

[17] David Caute, *Fanon* (London: Fontana/Collins, 1970).

[18] Omar Chaïr, 'Des Musulmans si tranquilles', *Historia Magazine*, 195 (1971) pp. 56–9.

[19] Richard Clutterbuck, *The Long Long War* (London: Cassell, 1967).

[20] Richard Cobb, *Terreur et Subsistances 1793–1795* (Paris: Librairie Clavreuil, 1964).

[21] Hubert Cole, *Fouché: The Unprincipled Patriot* (London: Eyre & Spottiswoode, 1971).

[22] Robert Conquest, *The Great Terror: Stalin's Purge of The Thirties* (London: Macmillan, 1968).

[23] T. P. Coogan, *I.R.A.* (London: Pall Mall, 1970).

[24] Lewis Coser, 'The Militant Collective: Jesuits and Leninists', *Social Research*, 40, 1 (Spring 1973) pp. 110–28.

[25] Yves Courrière, *La Guerre d'Algerie*: vol. 3, *L'Heure des colonels*, and vol. 4, *Les Feux du desespoir* (Paris: Fayard, 1970 and 1971).

[26] Bernard Crick, *Political Theory and Practice* (London: Allen Lane, 1972).

[27] Brian Crozier, *The Rebels: A Study of Post-War Insurrections* (London: Chatto & Windus, 1960).

[28] Alexander Dallin and George W. Breslauer, *Political Terror in Communist Systems* (Stanford, Calif.: Stanford University Press, 1970).

[29] M. Deanesly, *A History of the Medieval Church 590–1500* (London: Methuen, 1954).

[30] Regis Debray, *Revolution in the Revolution?* (Harmondsworth: Penguin, 1968).

[31] Bernal Díaz, *The Conquest of New Spain*, trans. with intro. by J. M. Cohen (Harmondsworth: Penguin, 1963).

[32] Martin Dillon and Denis Lehane, *Political Murder in Northern Ireland* (Harmondsworth: Penguin, 1973).

[33] Fyodor Dostoyevsky, *The Devils (The Possessed)*, trans. with intro. by David Magarshack (Harmondsworth: Penguin, 1962).

[34] H. Eckstein (ed.), *Internal War* (New York: Free Press, 1964).

[35] Gil Elliot, *Twentieth-Century Book of the Dead* (London: Allen Lane, 1972).

[36] Cynthia H. Enloe, *Ethnic Conflict and Political Development* (New York: Little Brown, 1973).

[37] Bernard B. Fall, *The Two Viet-Nams*, 2nd rev. edn (New York: Frederick A. Praeger, 1967).

[38]   Frantz Fanon, *The Wretched of the Earth*, trans. Constance Farrington (Harmondsworth: Penguin, 1967).

[39]   I. K. Feierabend, R. L. Feierabend and B. Nesvold, 'The Comparative Study of Revolution and Violence', *Comparative Politics*, 5, 3 (April 1973) pp. 393–424.

[40]   Helio Felgas, *The Terrorist Movements of Angola, Portuguese Guinea, Mozambique. Foreign Influence*, a translation of a series of articles from *Revista Militar* (Lisbon, 1966, translations on Africa, U.S. Dept of Commerce, Joint Publications Research Service (Washington, D.C., 1966).

[41]   L. Feuer, *The Conflict of Generations* (London: Heinemann, 1969).

[42]   M. R. D. Foot, *S.O.E. in France* (London: H.M.S.O., 1966).

[43]   Arnold Forster, 'Violence on the Fanatical Left and Right', *The Annals of the American Academy*, 364 (March 1966) pp. 141–8.

[44]   Sigmund Freud, *Civilization and Its Discontents*, rev. edn, ed. J. Strachey (London: Hogarth Press, 1963).

[45]   Sigmund Freud, *Psychopathology of Everyday Life*, trans. J. Strachey, new edn (London: Benn, 1966).

[46]   Erich Fromm, *The Fear of Freedom* (London: Routledge & Kegan Paul, 1942).

[47]   Roland Gaucher, *The Terrorists: From Tsarist Russia to the O.A.S.*, trans. from the French by Paula Spurlin (London: Secker & Warburg, 1968).

[48]   Julius Gould and William L. Kolb (eds), *A Dictionary of the Social Sciences* (Glencoe: UNESCO and the Free Press, 1964).

[49]   Hermann Graml, Hans Mommsen, Hans-Joachim Reichhardt, Ernst Wolf and F. L. Carsten, *The German Resistance to Hitler* (London: Batsford, 1970).

[50]   Donald Greer, *The Incidence of Terror during the French Revolution* (Cambridge, Mass.: Harvard University Press, 1935).

[51]   Feliks Gross, *The Seizure of Political Power* (New York: Philosophical Library, 1957).

[52]   Feliks Gross, 'Political Violence and Terror in 19th and 20th Century Russia and Eastern Europe', in *Assassination and Political Violence*, vol. 8 of *A Report to the National Commission on the Causes and Prevention of Violence*, ed. J. F. Kirkham, S. G. Levy and W. J. Crotty (Washington, D.C.: U.S. Govt Printing Office, 1969) pp. 421–76.

[53]   Che Guevara, *Guerrilla Warfare* (Harmondsworth: Penguin 1969).

[54] Ted Gurr, 'Psychological Factors in Civil Violence', *World Politics*, vol. 20, 2 (January 1968) pp. 245–78.

[55] J. B. S. Hardman, 'Terrorism', *Encyclopaedia of the Social Sciences*, ed. E. R. Seligman, 14 (New York: Macmillan, 1937) pp. 575–9.

[56] Otto Heilbrunn, *Partisan Warfare* (London: Allen & Unwin, 1962).

[57] Thomas Hobbes, *Leviathan* (London: Oxford University Press, 1947).

[58] Eric Hobsbawm, *Primitive Rebels* (Manchester: Manchester University Press, 1959).

[59] Eric Hobsbawm, *Bandits* (London: Weidenfeld & Nicolson, 1969).

[60] Simma Holt, *Terror in the Name of God: The Story of the Sons of Freedom Doukhobors* (Toronto/Montreal: McClelland & Stewart, 1964).

[61] Laurence Housman, *Terrorism by Ordinance* (London: The India League, n.d.).

[62] Samuel P. Huntington, *Political Order in Changing Societies* (New Haven: Yale University Press, 1968).

[63] Martha Crenshaw Hutchinson, 'The Concept of Revolutionary Terrorism', *The Journal of Conflict Resolution*, 16, 3 (September 1972) pp. 383–96.

[64] Ghiţa Ionescu, *Comparative Communist Politics* (London: Macmillan, 1972).

[65] James Joll, *The Anarchists* (London: Eyre & Spottiswoode, 1964).

[66] James Joll, 'Anarchism, a Living Tradition', in *Anarchism Today*, ed. D. Apter and J. Joll (London: Macmillan, 1971).

[67] *Journal of Air Law and Commerce*, 37 (Spring 1971) pp. 229–33.

[68] Herman Kahn, *On Escalation: Metaphors and Scenarios* (New York: Frederick A. Praeger, 1965).

[69] Josiah Kariuki, '*Mau Mau*' *Detainee* (London: Oxford University Press, 1963).

[70] Karl Kautsky, *The Dictatorship of the Proletariat*, intro. by John H. Kautsky (University of Michigan Press, 1964).

[71] Elie Kedourie (ed.), *Nationalism in Asia and Africa* (New York: Meridian Books, World Publishing Company, 1970).

[72] Frank Kitson, *Low Intensity Operations: Subversion, Insurgency and Peacekeeping* (London: Faber & Faber, 1971).

[73] Arthur Koestler, *Thieves in the Night* (London: Macmillan, 1946).

155

[74]   Prince Kropotkin, *Russkaia revolutsiia; anarkhizu* (London: Sonnenschein, 1907).

[75]   Thomas S. Kuhn, *The Structure of Scientific Revolutions* (Chicago: University of Chicago Press, 1970).

[76]   R. D. Laing and D. G. Cooper, *Reason and Violence: A Decade of Sartre's Philosophy 1950–60* (London: Tavistock, 1964).

[77]   H. T. Lambrick (ed. and trans.), *The Terrorist* (London: Ernest Benn, 1972).

[78]   George LeFebvre, *The French Revolution from its Origins to 1793* (London: Routledge & Kegan Paul, 1965).

[79]   Carl Leiden and Karl M. Schmitt, *The Politics of Violence* (New Jersey: Prentice-Hall, 1968).

[80]   V. I. Lenin, 'Partisan Warfare', *Proletari* (30 September 1906).

[81]   Bernard Lewis, *The Assassins. A Radical Sect in Islam* (London: Weidenfeld & Nicolson, 1967).

[82]   Gwynne Lewis, *Life in Revolutionary France* (London: Batsford, 1972).

[83]   S. M. Lipset, *Student Politics: Student Movements – Past and Present* (New York: Basic Books, 1967).

[84]   Albert Londres, *Terror in the Balkans*, with an appendix by L. Zarine (London: Constable, 1935).

[85]   Colin Lucas, *The Structure of the Terror: The Example of Javogues and the Loire* (London: Oxford University Press, 1972).

[86]   Niccolo Machiavelli, *The History of Florence* (London: Bohn's Standard Library, 1847) Book II, chap. 34.

[87]   Niccolo Machiavelli, *The Prince* and *The Discourses*, with an introduction by Max Lerner (New York: The Modern Library, 1950).

[88]   Norman I. Mackenzie (ed.), *Secret Societies* (London, Amsterdam: Aldus Books, 1967).

[89]   Edward McWhinney, *Hijacking of Aircraft*, Report of the Institut de Droit International, rapporteur E. McWhinney (1971).

[90]   Edward McWhinney, *The Illegal Diversion of Aircraft and International Law* (Hague Recueil, The Hague Academy of International Law, 1973).

[91]   Fred Majdalany, *State of Emergency: The Full Story of Mau Mau* (Boston: Houghton Mifflin, 1963).

[92]   Jay Mallin, *Terror in VietNam* (Princeton, N.J.: Van Nostrand, 1966).

[93]   Jay Mallin (ed.), *Terror and Urban Guerrillas: A Study of Tactics and Documents* (Coral Gables, Florida: University of Miami Press, 1971).

[94]   André Malraux, *La Condition humaine* (Paris: Gallimard, 1946).

[95]   André Malraux, *Le Triangle noir, Laclos, Goya, Saint-Just* (Paris: Gallimard, 1970).

[96]   Carlos Marighela, *For the Liberation of Brazil*, trans. John Butt and Rosemary Sheed (Harmondsworth: Penguin, 1971).

[97]   K. Marx and V. I. Lenin, *The Civil War in France: The Paris Commune* (New York: International Publishers, 1968).

[98]   Thomas Masaryk, *The Spirit of Russia*, vol. II (London: Allen & Unwin, 1919).

[99]   Maurice Merleau-Ponty, *Humanism and Terror*, trans. and annotated by J. O'Neill (Boston: Beacon Press, 1969).

[100] Charles Merriam, *Political Power* (New York: McGraw-Hill, 1934).

[101] Kenneth Minogue, *Nationalism* (London: Batsford, 1967).

[102] Baron Montesquieu, *De L'Esprit des Lois* (Paris: Librairie Garnier Frères, 1941) III, ch. 9, pp. 26–7.

[103] Baron Montesquieu, *Politique de Montesquieu*, ed. with intro. by Jean Ehrard (Paris: Armand Colin, 1965).

[104] Barrington Moore, Jr, *Terror and Progress – USSR. Some Sources of Change and Stability in the Soviet Dictatorship* (Cambridge, Mass.: Harvard University Press, 1966).

[105] Robert Moss, *Urban Guerrillas* (London: Maurice Temple Smith, 1972).

[106] Boris I. Nicolayevsky, *Asev, the Spy, the Russian Terrorist and Police Stool* (Garden City: Doubleday, 1934).

[107] Carlos Núñez, *The Tupamaros: Urban Guerrillas of Uruguay* (New York: Times Change Press, 1970).

[108] Sean O'Casey, *The Shadow of a Gunman*, in *Collected Plays*, vol. 1 (London: Macmillan, 1957) pp. 93–157.

[109] Nils Ørvik, 'Tanker Etter Kennedy-Mordet', *Samtiden*, 73 (1) (1964) pp. 64–70.

[110] Julian Paget, *Last Post: Aden 1964–67* (London: Faber, 1969).

[111] Bernard Pares, *A History of Russia*, rev. edn (London: Methuen, 1965).

[112] Peter Paret, *French Revolutionary Warfare from Indo-China to Algeria* (London: Pall Mall, 1964).

[113]   Leslie Paul, *The Age of Terror* (London: Faber, 1950).

[114]   Leopold Pospisil, *Kapauka Papuans and their Law* (Yale University Press, 1958).

[115]   Antonia Raeburn, *The Militant Suffragettes* (London: Michael Joseph, 1973).

[116]   *Revue militaire d'information* (Paris: February–March, 1957).

[117]   J. S. Roucek, 'I.M.R.O.', *Slavonic Encyclopedia* (New York: Philosophical Library, 1943) pp. 531–2.

[118]   J. S. Roucek, 'Sociological Elements of a Theory of Terror and Violence', *American Journal of Economics and Sociology*, 21, 2 (April 1962) pp. 165–72.

[119]   George Rudé, *Revolutionary Europe 1783–1815* (London: Collins, 1964).

[120]   Harry Sacher, *Israel: The Establishment of a State* (London: Weidenfeld & Nicolson, 1952).

[121]   Giovanni Sartori, 'Concept Misformation in Comparative Politics', *American Political Science Review*, 64 (1970) pp. 1033–53.

[122]   D. V. Segre and J. H. Adler, 'The Ecology of Terrorism', *Encounter*, 40, 2 (February 1973) pp. 17–24. Reprinted in *Survival* (Summer 1973).

[123]   Peter Singleton-Gates and Maurice Girodias, *The Black Diaries: An Account of Roger Casement's Life and Times with a Collection of his Diaries and Public Writings* (Paris: The Olympia Press, 1959).

[124]   Neil Smelser, *Theory of Collective Behaviour* (London: Routledge & Kegan Paul, 1962).

[125]   Anthony D. Smith, *Theories of Nationalism* (London: Duckworth, 1971).

[126]   George Sorel, *Reflections on Violence*, trans. T. E. Hulme and J. Roth (New York: Collier Books, 1961).

[127]   General A. Spiridovich, *Histoire du terrorisme russe*, trans. V. Lazarevski (Paris: Payot, 1930).

[128]   Alan B. Spitzer, *Old Hatreds and Young Hopes* (Cambridge, Mass.: Harvard University Press, 1971).

[129]   David Stafford, *Anarchism and Reformism* (London: Weidenfeld & Nicolson, 1972).

[130]   Max Stirner, *The Ego and his Own*, trans. S. T. Byington (London: Fifield, 1907).

[131]   Leo Strauss, *On Tyranny* (Glencoe, Ill.: Free Press, 1963).

[132]   Gaius Suetonius, *The Twelve Caesars*, trans. Robert Graves (Harmondsworth: Penguin, 1957).

[133]   Rex Taylor, *Michael Collins* (London: Hutchinson, 1958).

[134]   Sir Robert Thompson, *Revolutionary War in World Strategy 1945–1969* (London: Secker & Warburg, 1970).

[135]   William I. Thompson, *The Imagination of an Insurrection; Dublin, Easter 1916* (New York: Oxford University Press, 1967).

[136]   Thomas P. Thornton, 'Terror as a Weapon of Political Agitation', *Internal War*, ed. H. Eckstein (New York: Free Press, 1964) pp. 71–99.

[137]   Charles Tilly, 'Does Modernization Breed Revolution?', *Comparative Politics*, 5, 3 (April 1973) pp. 425–47.

[138]   Kostia Todoroff, 'The Macedonian Organisation Yesterday and Today', *Foreign Affairs*, 6 (1928) pp. 473–82.

[139]   Dinko Tomasic, 'The Ustasha Movement', *Slavonic Encyclopedia* (New York: Kennicat Press, 1949) pp. 1337–41.

[140]   L. Trotsky, *Terrorism and Communism: A Reply to Karl Kautsky*, with a Foreword by Max Shactman (Ann Arbor, Michigan: University of Michigan Press, 1963).

[141]   L. Trotsky, *Stalin, A Reappraisal* (London: MacGibbon & Kee, 1968).

[142]   P. J. Vatikiotis (ed.), *Revolution in the Middle East and Other Case Studies* (London: Allen & Unwin, 1972).

[143]   Jerży Waciorski, *Le Terrorisme politique* (Paris: A. Pedone, 1939).

[144]   Eugene V. Walter, 'Violence and the Process of Terror', *American Sociological Review*, 29, 2 (Spring 1964) pp. 248–57.

[145]   Eugene V. Walter, *Terror and Resistance: A Study of Political Violence with Case Studies of Some Primitive African Communities* (New York: Oxford University Press, 1969).

[146]   Eugene V. Walter, 'Politiche della violenza: da Montesquieu ai terroristi', *Communita*, 25, 163 (1971) pp. 7–30.

[147]   Denis A. Warner, *Out of the Gun* (London: Hutchinson, 1956).

[148]   Max Weber, *Essays in Sociology*, ed. and trans. H. H. Gerth and C. W. Mills (London: Routledge & Kegan Paul, 1947).

[149]   Simone Weil, *Oppression and Liberty* (London: Routledge & Kegan Paul, 1958).

[150]   Peter Weiss, *The Persecution and Assassination of Jean-Paul Marat: As performed by the Inmates of the Asylum of Charenton Under the Direction of the Marquis de Sade* (New York: Atheneum, 1972).

[151]   Paul Wilkinson, *Social Movement* (London: Pall Mall, 1971).

[152]   Paul Wilkinson, 'Three Questions on Terrorism', *Government and Opposition*, 8, 3 (Summer 1973) pp. 290–312.

[153]   Mervyn Williams (ed.), *Revolutions 1775–1830* (Harmondsworth: Penguin, 1971).

[154]   Marty Winch, *Psychology of the Wry* (publication details not available).

[155]   Bertram D. Wolfe, *Three Who Made a Revolution* (Harmondsworth: Penguin, 1966).

[156]   George Woodcock, *Anarchism: A History of Libertarian Ideas and Movements* (Cleveland: Meridian Books, World Publishing Company, 1962).

[157]   Frank Zimring, 'Is Gun Control Likely to Reduce Violent Killings?', *University of Chicago Law Review*, 35, 4 (Summr 1968) pp. 721–37.

322.42
W687p

3 1543 50014 5174

772303

DATE DUE

FE 22 79			
MY 18 79			
MY 12 80			
MR 23 81			
DE 08 81			

Cressman Library

Cedar Crest College
Allentown, Pa. 18104

OEMCO